the
chakhle
india
cookbook

the chakhle india cookbook

ADITYA BAL

Based on the
most popular food
show on
NDTV Good Times

westland ltd

Venkat Towers, 165, P.H. Road, Maduravoyal, Chennai 600 095
No. 38/10 (New No. 5), Raghava Nagar, New Timber Yard Layout, Bangalore 560 026
Survey No. A-9, II Floor, Moula Ali Industrial Area, Moula Ali, Hyderabad 500 040
23/181, Anand Nagar, Nehru Road, Santacruz East, Mumbai 400 055
4322/3, Ansari Road, Daryaganj, New Delhi 110 002

First published in India by westland ltd 2012

Text and pictures copyright © NDTV Lifestyle Ltd. 2012

All Rights Reserved

10 9 8 7 6 5 4 3 2 1

ISBN : 978-93-81626-58-0

Design, Illustrations and Typeset by Ishan Khosla Design
Typefaces used Aisha by Rozetta Type Foundry and Cronos MM by Monotype Foundry
Printed at Thomson Press India Ltd.

For
**Mom, Dad,
Pranav and Elena**

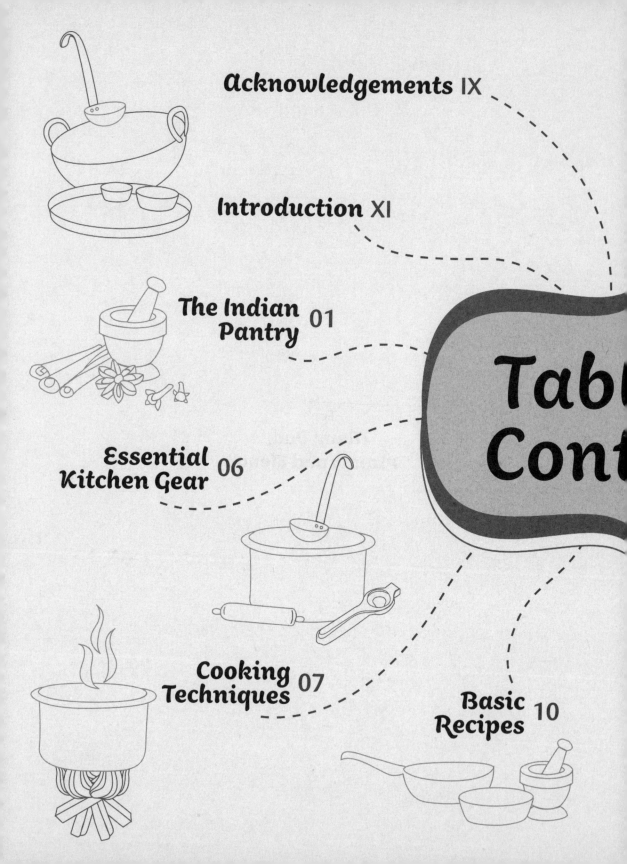

Tabl
Cont

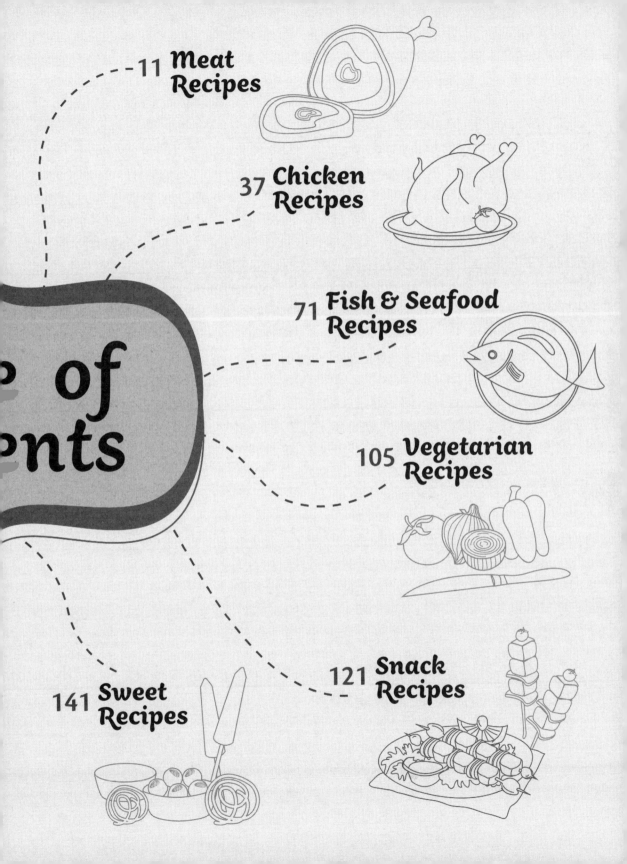

Acknowledgements

I'd like to dedicate this book to my family and loved ones. My mom and dad for always being amazingly supportive and loving. My brother for just being my best friend since the time he was old enough to walk and talk. My grandparents, especially my Nani, who was a source of inspiration to us all with her incredible cooking and baking that the entire family grew up around. I love you all and I am truly blessed to have such an amazing family!!

I would like to acknowledge all the people I've worked with over the last few years. Wendy and Maggie at 'Starcos Bar and Lounge' in Anjuna, Goa, for giving me my first kitchen stint and putting me on my path to learning: thank you so much. Sarjano at 'My Place' for his amazing schooling in how to cook with love and passion. Evan and Shaana Gwynn for always being there and the guidance and assistance I have continuously received whenever needed. My dear friend, the lovely Archana Vijaya for being so supportive when times were super tough… thank you again.

I'd like to say a huge thank you to Marrut Sikka, for his guidance and advice and for showing me the way forward and helping me find direction in the culinary arts.

Of course, none of this would have been possible without the amazing folks at NDTV Good Times. The one and only Monica Narula, Executive Producer, "Food Programming", for being a true friend, mentor, guide and the nicest person I have had the chance to work with ever. Your faith and belief in me has been a constant source of support and inspiration… Thank you for giving me the amazing opportunity to do what I truly love. You are a true friend and inspiration to us all!!

The lovely Seema Chandra, Tanu Ganguly Yadav, Asavari Capoor. For all the amazing and brilliant effort at every stage of the show's production and for being the nicest and friendliest people to work with.

I would also like to thank Shibani Khanna, Channel Head at NDTV Good Times for giving me the chance to be part of the NDTV family, for the support, love and guidance that I have been truly lucky to receive. Thank you so much!! Thanks to Smeeta Chakrabarti, CEO, NDTV Lifestyle Ltd. for the advice, belief and faith she reposed in me over the last few years, and under whose leadership the channel grows from strength to strength.

Thank you to all those who have had a hand in producing the show: Amitabh Gautam and Puneet Gautam at 'Dreamcatchers', as also Anant, Raj, Honey, and Monika Kala. Thank you guys!! I am also thankful to Monia Pinto and the entire team at 'Face TV' for believing in the show and going through so much to help make it possible.

Finally I'd like to thank everyone who has watched the series and with such intent and accepted it, and loved it for what it is. Without your support and constant encouragements, none of this would have happened. Thank you all so much!!

Also, a big thank you to all the amazing people I have had the chance to meet on my travels. The chefs, cooks, families, officials and generally everyone who has helped us in doing what we set out to do. The people of India are truly amazing, extremely generous with their time and always ready to help, no matter what. I have learnt a lot from all of them, a learning experience of a lifetime, and one that can only continue to get even more interesting!!

A very special thank you to Rachel Tanzer, whose continued belief in the book has made it possible to make it a reality. Your amazing effort and guidance has been invaluable and I hope we can collaborate on many a project in the future. A word of thanks to everyone at Westland for believing in the project and for all the great work they put into the book.

Introduction

My first real memories of food are probably those of kiladis, a stringy mountain sheep's milk cheese made by shepherds in the mountains of Gulmarg, a picture perfect hill station in Kashmir. I was all of three maybe, and I remember the shepherds would come to our little hotel, 'Snow View', which was run by my mother and father in the 1970s, and each day, after my mother had bathed and fed me breakfast, they would take me out with them on their grazing trips, and give me kiladis to take home. Even now, its chewy, slightly stringy texture, a creamy-sour flavour, sprinkled with salt and a little red chilli is vividly etched in my mind. Though I don't know if they gave me any with the chilli at that age.

Growing up in Kashmir was an absolute dream for any kid. It was an idyllic setting and an equally idyllic childhood: lots of open spaces to play about and greenery everywhere. Our family had always loved food and I remember watching my mother, Anila, cooking the day's meals early in the morning before packing me off to school each day. Meat and rice were staples, being the favourite of all Kashmiris, and it was always sheep's meat, not goat's, which had a really meaty and robust aroma and was always nice and fatty. My family is from Punjab and hence there were also other staple dishes like saag paneer, one of my favourites to date, sukhe aloo, paranthas on Sundays and gajar ka halwa or gajrela. My mother also possessed a formidable arsenal of continental dishes in her repertoire, handed down and taught by her mother, my Naniji.

A legendary cook and baker in her own right, my grandmother is probably indirectly responsible for my own talent as a cook; her countless handwritten recipe books still inspire me. I firmly believe that my becoming a cook has a lot to do with her natural talent as a cook, and it's been passed down to me through generations. I remember travelling to Delhi each winter for vacations and her cooking up a feast for us on a regular basis. There were roasts and hams, pasta and simply done vegetables, bakes and of course, her forte, cakes. Each birthday I would be treated to something new and fantastic, a chocolate house, a car, an aeroplane cake, a fireman cake with gems for buttons. Freshly baked cookies and ginger biscuits were always stocked in seemingly endless supply. It was like being transported into a fascinating new world, an absolute food heaven. I think at a very early age, I was amazed by food in all its glory. I thank my Nani, may God rest her soul, for being the perfect grandma, always treating her family to life's tastiest delights. She cooked with love and the only way she knew. Thank you, Naniji.

Then, there was the wazwan, the legendary wedding feast of the Kashmiri people. At least twice a year, we would be invited to this ritual of feasting. There would be music and traditional dance, and of course the wazas, meaning master cooks, busy churning out one delicacy after the other. The meal would be served on a traami, a large heavy plate for four. A mountain of rice, no exaggeration, would be served with a few dry items like kababs, tabaq maaz (ribs cooked in milk and then deep fried in ghee) and a walnut chutney. Then, one course after another, the onslaught would begin. The sequence was perfectly timed and in keeping with tradition. Being a small boy, I remember eating as much as I possibly could, watching in amazement as men sat quietly and finished an entire traami, single-handedly, and then passing out on my dear mother's lap. Full, happy, and satisfied. Little did I know then that I was witnessing the ritual of community feasting, and the food was a way to bring people together. Everyone was united in the joyous act of celebration through the partaking of "heavenly food".

In sharp contrast to traditional feasts and delicious home cooked Indian cuisine, were my parents' parties. Often, they and their group of friends would get together for a "pot luck", the idea being that everyone brought one dish to the party, there-by reducing the work load on any one person in the group. As Kashmir was known for its organic quality of sheep's meat, wild morels (which seemed to grow just about anywhere), strawberries, fantastic trout and many such exotic produce, these menus somehow always consisted of continental dishes: roast baby lamb, hot jacket potatoes with fresh butter, fresh wild mushrooms cooked in butter with fresh herbs from the garden, and lots of fresh fruit with the most luscious cream I have ever had. Each household seemed to have their staple dishes. Dishes that have remained in my memory till date. I feel very fortunate to have had such a great childhood, growing up with my younger brother, Pranav, and loving parents, Rakesh and Anila, surrounded by natural beauty and living a simple life.

In 1989, aged thirteen, all that would change forever. Six months later, with normal life having come to an abrupt halt and militancy taking over life in Kashmir, my family had no choice but to move to Delhi, and I got sent away to a boarding school. I found myself at the Lawrence School, Sanawar, a 160 year-old institution set in the hills of Himachal Pradesh, an hour's drive from Chandigarh. I was fourteen, and luckily had been able to clear the difficult entrance test to this great school, just as schools had shut in Kashmir. Life in a boarding school was an everyday battle for survival. My batch was the juniormost and we always got the rough end of the stick from everyone. It was a hardy and disciplined life, we had to do everything, and try to do it well. Studies, sports, extra curricular activities were all equally important. The school was co-educational, and there was always plenty of inspiration on hand, always some girl we would want to impress.

The most important aspect of school life perhaps was food. It was everything to us, and we would beg, borrow, fight and steal to get that extra little bit. In the dorms, it was used as currency. For instance, "my share of butter for a whole week in exchange for Maggi noodles tonight". If you wanted to show your feelings for a girl, you could send her your first share, which meant you gave up your ration of say, mutton curry at lunch, and sent it to the girl you wanted to impress! Or, if there was a senior who was generally making life hell, you would try and get him, or her in some cases, some "extras", an effort that would always go down well with them. I made my way through five years of school, and during this time, learning the sheer importance of simple food. Along with the quality education I received during my time at school, maybe the most valuable one, was to respect and value food. Its power to sustain and feed, impress and pacify, trade and protect. Anything was possible with food. It had a language and world all of its own.

The next twelve years of my life were spent between going to college, and walking the ramp as a professional model. I even managed a two-year stint trying to get that all important break as an actor in Bollywood. I had moved to Mumbai in 1999 and it was now 2006. Somehow, my career as a model was at its end, and the acting also wasn't really going anywhere. I was frustrated with work and life in general and had no clue what to do with anything. It was during this phase of my life, that I decided one evening, sitting at home, waiting for yet another delayed film schedule to start, to venture into the kitchen and cook something. Anything. Out of sheer boredom and stressed out to the core, I got into the kitchen, called a friend for a recipe for lamb chops I remembered eating at his place, and started. They were not the most brilliant chops in the world, but they were my creation, and I was thrilled. My girlfriend at the time Archana, who served as an inspiration for countless number of dishes to follow, and to whom I am eternally grateful, ate the meal and was full of encouragement. Clearly it wasn't a complete disaster, and I went to bed satisfied with what I had done for the first time in many moons.

After that night, with not having much real work to do, I found myself in the kitchen more and more, reading recipe books and trying out recipes. To my utter delight, and to the delight of a few close friends, who were to be my guinea pigs, most of what one cooked and baked (baking is one of my favourite parts of all cookery), turned out well. A few months of cooking down the line, and it was all I would think of and do. I had somehow found my talent, and that was to cook. I don't know what it was that made me decide to try and make it my calling, maybe it was the desire to have a little more control over one's own destiny, and the satisfaction I had when I saw my friends happy after a meal, but I decided that I was going to take a chance with cooking as a career.

Acting on this deep desire and instinct, I packed my bags and headed to the only place where I knew I could get the chance to work in a restaurant kitchen, without any formal training: Goa. I managed to convince my dear friends, Maggie and Wendy, who own and run the 'Starcos Bar and Lounge' in Anjuna, to let me work in their kitchen. Seeing me so full of passion for cooking, I guess they finally decided that they would risk letting me loose in their simple restaurant that served up a typical Goan menu with everything from breakfast, to steaks and pasta, to Goan and Portuguese cuisine. Never before had I felt so exhilarated with my work. After a six month stint at the restaurant, and with a lot of basic knowledge under my belt, I moved on from 'Starcos Bar and Lounge' to a fine Italian restaurant called 'My Place' run by an eccentric Italian master chef, Sarjano and his son, Amore. Here I worked for a season and I am very grateful to them for teaching me the nuances of simple yet delicious Italian cuisine, cooked with love and from the heart. I also put in a season-long stint after that with my dear friends and top chef, Evan Gwynn and his wife, Shaana, at their beautiful restaurant in Baga where the food was fine dine Mediterranean and classic French.

Living and working in Goa meant that when I was not at the restaurant, I was cooking at home, experimenting with ingredients and techniques, flavours and cuisines. Goa is a cook's paradise, with fantastic fresh produce and a knowledgeable seller and customer, the place revolves around good food and drink. The multiple nationalities of the people working there coupled with the perfect environment to cook, according to me, makes Goa one of the best places to cook in our country. It inspires the cook and the diner alike, and this fuels a desire to be creative and push the envelope in the kitchen a bit. I was lucky to have had such a great start to my culinary career.

By now I was fully charged up and knew that I could more than just survive the rigors of the professional kitchen. I could excel in this field, and with that belief, I left for Mumbai after a span of a year and a half. I was looking around for work in a professional kitchen in Mumbai and Delhi for quite a while, and trying to figure out a way of turning my passion for cooking into a career and livelihood. I didn't get a very favourable response from Mumbai for some reason, and I think it was because people didn't believe that I could really cut it in a professional kitchen. After a few months of asking around for work, I realized that the only way to actually get going was to try and start up my own venture. I also realized that I didn't have sufficient experience at the time to really make a success of whatever I was planning to do. The restaurant business is unforgiving to say the least, and you need to have a few years of experience under your belt, before you can even think of starting up your own.

With no real luck in Mumbai, I went home to my family in Delhi, hoping to find some work there, through family and friends' contacts. A week or so later I found myself sitting at Marrut Sikka's 'Magique' in Delhi, asking him for advice on how to go about things, when he suggested that I go and meet Monica Narula at NDTV Good Times. At the time, he was hosting a cookery show for them, and he felt that it would be the best way to take things forward, for me.

It's been almost four years since I first met Monica Narula, Executive Producer, NDTV Good Times, "Food Programming", a wonderful person with a great vision and understanding of the field of lifestyle TV, and who has now become a good friend and guide to me over the years. I told her about my experience and she said that they would like to screen test me for upcoming shows on the channel. A couple of weeks later, a camera crew came home to my folks' place in Gurgaon, and I cooked and demonstrated a Goan classic, Pomfret Reachado with a fresh mango salsa. I thought it went pretty well, and hoped that something would work out soon.

Then one day, I got a call from Monica, saying that they really liked the test, and that they could have something for me on the cookery show front. I can't tell you how excited and happy I was after speaking to her! Finally, I was going to get a chance to showcase my skills. I headed to Delhi a few days later and met with the amazing team at the channel. I was told that the show would be on regional Indian cuisine, and we would be starting off with a pilot episode, in Lucknow.

From that first day of shooting, to four wonderful seasons later, I have been very fortunate and privileged to have had the amazing opportunity of travelling the country, learning, cooking and experiencing the vast and endlessly diverse culture and cuisines of India. It's been a fantastic learning process for me and has helped me grow tremendously as a person and as a cook. I firmly believe that the best education for a cook is to travel, eat and experience different cuisines and cultures. Experiencing the little nuances, traditions and local ingredients that shape the cuisine of a place first hand, is a great way to better understand any cuisine and culture.

The Chakh Le India Cookbook is my first, and it is based on my travels and culinary exploration of the first three seasons of the show. It is primarily a recipe book which has the best recipes that you may have seen on the show. Though the recipes are mostly traditional, they are essentially my version of authentic regional dishes from around India. There are also sections on the Indian Pantry, Essential Kitchen Gear, Cooking Techniques, and Basic Recipes. Some of the recipes may seem very long and fairly complex, once a few basic principles of Indian cookery is mastered, Indian cooking becomes a lot simpler than it seems. As with all cookery, it has to be instinctive and done with lots of fun. The recipes in this book are not set in stone, so they can be improvized and recreated with alternative flavour profiles. It's easy once one has had a little practice in the kitchen.

I hope everybody enjoys reading and cooking from this wonderful book of recipes and most importantly share what I feel immensely, a great love for food and cooking with family, friends and loved ones. The joy of cooking is one of the most satisfying for the cook and the diner, here's to spreading lots of joy, and good food. Happy cooking!!

ADITYA BAL
July 2012

The Indian Pantry

A well stocked and organized pantry or store cupboard goes a long way towards better and more varied cooking. The essential ingredients, aromatics, spices and grains that are required to stock an Indian kitchen are quite vast, and while it may not be possible to stock every local ingredient across all of India's regional cuisines, it is possible to store the basic elements of the cuisine in a kitchen.

For organizational and restocking purposes, the ingredients and components have been divided into groups based on the type of ingredient, along with how they can be used.

AROMATICS

Ginger, garlic and onions: These aromatics form the base or the Holy Trinity of Indian cuisine and are used in several different ways and combinations to achieve a wide array of flavour profiles and effects in the finished dish. Added whole or roughly chopped into large pieces to hot oil, they release a delicate, aromatic sweetness and pungency to the dish. They can be chopped fine, sliced thin, dry-roasted and ground to a coarse or fine paste; or fried in oil and then ground to a paste with vinegar or water. Ginger and garlic form the base for innumerable spice pastes.

Onions too, are commonly used in spice pastes throughout India and to thicken gravies.

Spring onions: They can be chopped fine and used as a garnish. They can also be fried or dry-roasted and ground with other ingredients to make a fresh green spice paste or masala.

CHILLIES

Dried red chillies: Many different varieties are used in Indian cuisine ranging from mild and smoky to very hot and pungent. A pantry should stock two to three varieties for regular use. The most commonly used are Kashmiri, Byadagi, Guntur and the small, round Bor chilli. Kashmiri chillies are used for their colour and smokiness; Byadagi have a mild heat, whereas Guntur are fiery hot. They can be used whole, broken, dry-roasted and ground coarse or fine to make a powder. They are also ground with other ingredients to make spice pastes and masalas.

Green chillies: These too are found in several varieties in India, ranging from very mild to very hot. They are used in many different ways to achieve a wide range of flavour profiles: whole or split for mild heat, chopped large for more intensity, chopped fine for even more flavour and heat, dry-roasted and ground to make aromatic pastes with other ingredients.

Red chillies: The fresh, small ones have an intense, lingering heat and are mostly used to make chutneys and pickles. They can be used whole to flavour a cooking medium or chopped for an intense and hot hit. They are dry-roasted or fried in oil and ground to a fine paste to make a red chilli paste, or with other spices and ingredients to make a hot spice paste.

DAIRY

Butter: Both salted and white butter are used as cooking mediums in Indian recipes and also to add flavour and colour to several dishes.

Cream: Cream is used extensively in Indian cuisine. It is used as a medium for a curry on its own, or added to a curry to give it a rich flavour and a creamy, luxurious texture and consistency. It is more commonly used in North Indian cuisine than in the south of India.

Ghee or clarified butter: It has a lovely, rich, nutty aroma and flavour with a very high smoke point, making ghee the ideal medium for browning, searing and to bhuno or fry a masala. It should be used sparingly to add richness and depth to a dish. It is largely used in biryani and rice dishes and is indispensable while making most Indian sweets or mithai.

Milk: Milk is used as a medium for gravies. It can be used in place of or in combination with cream, for a lighter effect. It is commonly infused with saffron and other aromatic spices, to flavour a biryani and other rice dishes too. Reduced milk solids or khoya, forms the base for several Indian sweets and to thicken the gravies of some Mughlai dishes.

Yoghurt or curd: The Indian version has a high water content, unlike its Greek counterpart which is thick and creamy. In India, it needs to be whisked thoroughly to blend the curd with the whey and make it creamy and smooth. It is used as a medium for many meat curries and vegetable dishes and with aromatics and spices as a marinade for meat, fish, chicken and vegetables.

DRY INGREDIENTS

Flours: A pantry should stock wheat flour or atta and refined white flour or maida at all times. Both are used to make a wide range of Indian breads and even some desserts and sweets. Semolina, sooji or rava, is used in many Indian dishes as well.

Lentils or dals: It is recommended to stock several varieties, as they are used extensively across India according to regional preferences along with red kidney beans, chickpeas and so on.

Rice: Stock the long-grained basmati variety as well as a good short-grained one in the pantry.

HERBS

Fresh coriander: Fresh coriander is chopped fine or rough and used as a garnish on most dishes. It can be added fresh or fried in oil to any spice paste or masala.

Fresh dill: Dill is used to flavour fish and other seafood curries. It is also used to make a delicate marinade for fried fish and seafood dishes.

Mint: Often used as a garnish for a curry, pulao, biryani and salad, mint can be ground in a spice paste too. Dried mint leaves are used extensively in Kashmiri dishes.

OILS

Groundnut oil: It has a nutty aroma and flavour and is great for frying.

Mustard oil: Owing to its wonderful pungency, mustard oil needs to be burnt or smoked before using it in a dish. This oil is essential to Kashmiri and Bengali cuisines. It is also used to add a robust character to a dish.

Refined oil: This is a vegetable oil and has almost no flavour or aroma.

SOURING AGENTS

Dry mango and raw mango: Known as amchoor, dried mango has a lovely, sharp, sour and mildly sweet flavour. It can be ground to a fine powder to add a delicious, fresh sourness to any dish.

Whole green or raw mangoes are widely used to flavour fish and other seafood curries along India's west coast. It can be cooked and ground to make a thick, sour purée as well.

Kokum: Kokum has an almost balsamic, sweet-sour, tannic flavour with a salty finish and is mostly used in its dry, black-brown rind form. It is added to curries and lentil dishes to give them a lovely sweet-sour tang. It can also be ground with other ingredients to make a spice paste for any fish or seafood recipe.

Limes and lemons: Both are used extensively in Indian cookery. The juice is mainly used to add acidity and freshness to a dish. The two can be used along with other ingredients in marinades or to moisten and liven up a spice paste. It is commonly used to lift out the flavours of countless dishes.

Tamarind: This sticky, dark brown fruit is intensely sour and mildly sweet on the finish. It is most commonly used to make a thick extract when dissolved in warm water. It is also used to add depth and a sour kick to curries. Tamarind extract can be added to spice pastes and several marinades. It is generally used along with a little jaggery to balance out its sourness.

Vinegars: Several local varieties are used in Indian cuisine—malt, sugarcane, jaggery, tamarind and coconut being some of them. Each has a different level of acidity and sweetness. Some are very sour and pungent, while others are mild. They are used in aromatic pastes, spice pastes, marinades or on their own to add a tangy kick and depth to a dish. They are an important preservative in several pickles and preserves.

SPICES

Bay leaf: With its delicate wood-spiced aroma and flavour, bay leaf is mainly used dried in Indian cuisine and sometimes whole to flavour rice dishes or curries. It can be broken for a slightly more pronounced flavour, dry-roasted and ground with other spices to make garam masala powders and several complex, intensely flavoured spice pastes.

Black pepper: Widely used throughout India, black pepper provides heat and pungency to innumerable dishes. It can be used whole for a delicate accent, ground coarse or fine, dry-roasted and added to garam masala powders and, ground with other ingredients to make fiery, hot spice pastes.

Brown cardamom: This strong, woody, astringent spice has an intense aroma and flavour. It is used whole, fried in oil or added to a curry for a delicate flavour and aroma. Brown cardamom is also dry-roasted and ground coarsely or fine as an ingredient of garam masala or with other ingredients into a spice paste. While grinding, the outer husk should be discarded and only the seeds used.

Cassia bark: This is the outer bark of the cinnamon tree and has a sweet, slightly bitter, wood-spice flavour and aroma. It is used whole to temper and flavour cooking mediums as well as ground fine in many garam masalas and spice pastes.

Cloves: Cloves are really sharp and hot with a menthol flavour. They are used whole to impart their delicate heat to a dish when fried in a hot cooking medium. They can be ground for a very intense, sharp heat or dry-roasted and ground into a spice paste.

Coriander seeds: These herby, grassy seeds can be used whole, toasted and broken in half, coarsely ground or ground to a fine powder. They are not only used to make fresh garam masala powders, but also used extensively in spice pastes.

Cumin seeds: One of the most commonly used spices in Indian cuisine, cumin seeds are used whole, ground coarsely or fine. It is used in several spice pastes as well. Cumin seeds are used extensively for tempering a variety of meat, lentil and vegetable dishes.

Curry leaves: They have a very delicate, musky, citrus flavour and aroma. They are indispensable to South Indian cooking. Used whole, they have almost no flavour but when fried whole in a hot cooking medium, they have a rich, fragrant aroma. They can be used whole or dry-roasted or fried in oil and ground into a spice paste.

Dried ginger: It is called saunth in North India and has a fairly intense citrus pungency. Dried ginger is generally ground finely to flavour several Kashmiri and Punjabi dishes. Whole dried ginger can be dry-roasted and ground to a fine powder on its own or to make a fragrant garam masala powder when ground with other spices.

Aniseed: This spice is also known as choti saunf. It has a fresh, liquorice, citrus aroma and flavour. It is used whole, dry roasted and ground fine for a more assertive flavour or ground with other ingredients in many spice pastes. It is also used as a natural mouth freshener.

Fenugreek seeds: These have a bitter, astringent flavour and are mostly used whole to temper several South Indian dishes. They can be dry-roasted and ground into curry and sambhar powders or along with other ingredients to lend a mild, bitter depth to spice pastes.

Green cardamoms: Citrusy, fresh and aromatic, green cardamoms are used in various ways. They are used whole to infuse any dish with its delicate flavour or crackled in hot oil to release their aroma. They are also ground coarsely or fine, with other spices in garam masala powders or in complex spice pastes and marinades. These are also used to flavour rice dishes and sweets.

Mace: Mace is the outer kernel of nutmeg. This warm spice is peppery and woody in its flavour but milder than nutmeg in intensity. It can be used whole or crackled in oil to flavour rice dishes. It is also powdered fine, or dry-roasted whole with other warm spices in garam masalas, or with other ingredients in a spice paste or marinade.

Mustard seeds: Sharp, pungent and bitter in flavour, mustard seeds are used widely in a number of recipes. They are a common pickling spice, used whole or ground fine to give a bitter-sour flavour. They are crackled whole in hot oil to temper a dish, or dry-roasted and ground into sambhar powders, South Indian curry powders and robust spice pastes.

Nutmeg: This very strong, woody and earthy spice has a persistent heat and pungency to it. Used to add depth and intensity to any spice powder or paste, it is mainly used grated or ground fine and in fairly small quantities.

Saffron: This musky, rich, floral and aromatic spice is the most expensive in the world. Used rather sparingly to infuse milk, cream or any other liquid with its colour and aroma, it adds flavour and colour to biryanis or pulao, and several other Mughlai recipes as well. It is extensively used to make Indian sweets or mithai and desserts.

Turmeric: Perhaps the most commonly used spice in Indian cuisine, turmeric has a complex, rich, intensely citrus, woody flavour and aroma to it. It is generally used in powder form to add depth, colour and flavour to a dish. It is also used to combine various other spices in several masala powders and pastes.

OTHER COMMON INGREDIENTS

Fresh coconut: Use it grated to garnish dishes or fried /dry-roasted and ground with other ingredients to make spice pastes. Fresh coconut milk and coconut cream are used as a medium for curries in many dishes in South Indian cooking.

Jaggery: It is used mostly to balance tamarind or other souring agents in a variety of recipes. It has a great depth to its sweetness which in turns adds layers to any finished dish.

Tomatoes: They are chopped coarse or fine, sliced or puréed.

Essential Kitchen Gear

Professional kitchens may need to use plenty of complicated equipment to produce a wide variety of dishes with efficiency, but in reality all one needs to cook great food are a few basic pieces of equipment and a couple of gadgets. Here is a list of basic kitchen tools that are required while cooking at home:

CHOPPING BOARDS

Heavy wooden block
Heavy plastic board

KNIVES

A good quality heavy chef's knife
Pairing knife
Bread knife
Boning/filleting knife
Sharpening steel
Kitchen shears

MACHINERY

Oven
Gas or charcoal grill
Steamer
Good quality stove/gas range or
    burners

PEELERS AND GRATERS

Box grater
Speed peeler
Microplane grater/zester

POTS AND PANS

A couple of heavy non-stick
    pans in different sizes
Heavy cast iron or stainless
    steel frying pan
Wok/kadhai
Sauté pans
Saucepans; small and large
Braising pan/casserole dish
Omelette pan

SMALL WARES

Balloon whisk
Spatulas
Stainless steel mixing bowls
Cranked turner
Meat tongs
Cooking spoons/paddles
Measuring spoons
Ladles
Colander
Sieves/ fine and coarse
Tea strainer
Stick blender
Mixer grinder
Mortar and pestle
Weighing scale

Cooking Techniques

Baghar: This is a process of flavouring a cooking medium. Spices, aromatics or any other ingredients are fried in a hot cooking medium, till they have crackled and released their flavours and aromas into the medium. They are then discarded and the flavoured medium is used.

Bhunao: This is a fundamental cooking technique used in Indian cuisine. Spices, herbs and aromatics are sautéed over high heat, till they are toasted and intensely aromatic. A little liquid is then added to deglaze the pan and blend the ingredients well. Once most of the liquid evaporates, the process is repeated, till the aromatic spice base is homogenous and the oil rises to the top, signifying that the masala is properly cooked.

Boiling: Food is immersed in water or any other liquid and cooked at boiling point. Boiling provides a very intense and violent heat to the food, so meats and most vegetables are actually simmered at a lower temperature to cook them through to tenderness while maintaining their texture.

Braising: Braising combines the techniques of dry and moist heat. Large, whole pieces of food, usually meat or poultry are first seared and browned in a hot pan and then simmered along with aromatics, vegetables and liquid (usually stock, water, wine or a juice), till they are fork-tender. The food is cooked at a very low temperature, allowing the collagen in the meat to turn to gelatine, thus making it very tender. Since the food cooks slowly, a rich, flavoursome sauce or gravy is formed automatically, which is then clarified and reduced to concentrate the flavours and served with the braised food.

Concentration of flavours: It simply means that a finished dish or ingredient has an extremely intense flavour either of that ingredient or of the combination of ingredients cooked together.

Deep-frying: Food is cooked by immersing it in hot fat. The fat can be oil, butter, ghee or any other animal fat. Deep-frying is used to quicken the process of cooking. The food is usually coated in a batter to protect it from the direct heat of the oil. Deep-fried foods have a characteristic crisp golden exterior, while the interior remains moist and succulent.

Double-boiling: This technique is commonly used when melting or cooking delicate dishes or foods such as custards, chocolates and egg-based emulsions such as hollandaise sauce. The food is put in a metal or copper bowl, which in turn is placed over a slightly larger vessel that is half filled with boiling water. As the steam rises and hits the bowl above, it gently heats the ingredients, cooking or melting them in the process. It is a great way of providing gentle heat to any ingredient that is being cooked.

Dry-roasting: Spices, herbs, aromatics or vegetables are roasted in a hot, dry pan or in the oven without any oil or fat to help release their natural oils and intensify their flavour and aroma.

Grilling: Small pieces of food are cooked over a glowing, hot source. Generally, the food is first marinated or seasoned and cooked over a grill heated by coal, wood, gas or electricity. Grilling is ideal for tender and fast cooking of meat, and most vegetables. The food is first seared very close to the heat source, and then moved further away to cook it through to perfection. Grilling over wood and coal gives the food a lovely smoky flavour and grill marks which makes the food look great too.

Pan-frying: Medium to large pieces of food are cooked by frying in a hot pan that has been coated with a simmering cooking medium. Chops, chicken breasts, fish fillets, steaks, etc. can all be pan-fried to perfection. The food is first seared at a high heat to brown and caramelize the sugars, then the temperature is turned down and the food is cooked to the desired extent.

Poaching: Food is cooked by immersing it in simmering liquid at a very low temperature so as to keep its structure and texture intact. It is generally used while cooking tender cuts of meat, poultry, fish and other seafood, as well as fruits and eggs.

Reduction: A liquid or any other ingredient is reduced in quantity to concentrate the flavour, for example, a red wine reduction or simply reducing a curry by one-third to concentrate its flavours.

Sautéing: This is a French term which means to jump. Small pieces of food are tossed in a hot pan with a heated cooking medium. Sautéing helps food to cook quickly, while retaining their flavours and textures. There are several different ways to sauté, but the basic principle is to toss the food to cook it quickly and evenly.

Searing: The exterior of the food is caramelized by subjecting it to very high temperatures. This causes the sugars in the food to caramelize, thereby giving it a lovely brown crust, packed with flavours. Searing usually precedes a main cooking technique like frying, sautéing, roasting or grilling.

Shallow-frying: Food is first fried in a hot pan with enough fat to immerse one side of it and then it is flipped over and the second side is fried. This method uses less oil than deep-frying and also gives the food a crisp golden exterior and moist interior. However, food need not be battered when shallow-frying, unless the recipe calls for it.

Simmering: Here, the food is cooked in a simmering liquid (below boiling point) for a certain amount of time, till it is tender.

Spice paste: A spice paste is a combination of aromatics, herbs, spices and other ingredients, such as tomatoes, coconut and chillies, that are dry-roasted or fried in hot oil and then ground to a paste. Spice pastes can be really simple in flavour or very complex, depending on the combination of ingredients used to make them. The advantages of a spice paste are the depth of its flavour, a smooth texture of the resulting gravy or masala and a consistency of flavour each time a specific amount is used.

Steaming: This is a technique whereby food is cooked in the hot steam generated by a boiling liquid. It is generally used to cook light foods such as dim-sums, fish fillets, vegetables and also to make custards. The food is enclosed in a steamer and cooks through in the gentle but intense heat generated by the steam. This is a great technique, as steaming not only retains almost all the nutrients of the food, it also makes the food tender and moist.

Stewing: This is similar to braising, except that the food is generally cut into small pieces. These pieces are then seared if the recipe calls for it, or cooked without searing for a lighter dish. Aromatics and vegetables chopped into medium-sized pieces are then added to the pan along with the cooking liquid (usually stock, water, wine or a juice) and the food, either meat or vegetables, is simmered, till tender. The sauce in this case is generally thinner than that of a braise.

Tempering or tadka: Here, spices and aromatics are fried in a hot cooking medium till they crackle and release their aromas and flavours into the cooking medium. Tempering can be done either in the initial stages or towards the end of the cooking process.

Wet-roasting: Spices, herbs and aromatics are roasted in oil or butter to intensify their flavour.

Yakhni: This technique creates a rich flavourful broth or stock by simmering meat or poultry in hot liquid while par-cooking the ingredients. The ingredients are boiled in water along with salt and or whole spices till it is cooked and a rich flavoursome stock is released. The meat or poultry is then added to the gravy along with the stock and the dish cooks over very low heat, till done to perfection.

Cooking Techniques

Basic Recipes

Coconut milk: Carefully break open a coconut and remove the flesh from the shell using a blunt knife. Chop into small pieces and put them into a grinder. Add enough warm water to cover and grind, till it forms a coarse paste. Transfer the ground coconut into a strainer and squeeze the thick extract into a bowl. Repeat the process with the residue in the strainer a couple of times, to get the medium and thin milk. Discard the final residue in the strainer.

Ginger-garlic paste: Peel the ginger and garlic and dry-roast them, till they are fragrant. Transfer to a mortar and add a little salt to act as an abrasive. Grind to the desired consistency. A little water or vinegar can be added for a looser or smoother consistency.

Kokum extract: Put some kokum into a bowl and add a cup of warm water. Rub the kokum gently with your fingers to release its flavour. Leave to infuse for about 30 minutes. Strain and reserve the extract.

Tamarind extract: Soak a handful of tamarind pulp in a little warm water for 10 minutes. Squeeze it with your hands, till all the dark brown pulp has been loosened. Hold a strainer over another bowl and strain the thick pulp through it, pressing out as much pulp as possible. Discard the seeds and the fibre, stir the extract well and use.

Tomato purée: Put the tomatoes in boiling water for a few minutes, shock under cold running water and remove the skins. Chop the flesh coarsely and blitz in a blender to get a smooth purée. The purée can also be strained for a smoother, more refined version.

Whisked curd: Whisk fresh curd with a fork or whisk, till well blended and smooth.

Meat

RECIPES

Rogan Josh
Pg 30

Galawati Kabab
(Melt-in-the-Mouth Kabab)

3 SERVINGS

These Mughlai kababs are legendary because they just melt in the mouth. They owe their famous silky texture to the pounding of the mixture, till it is pasty, which is then mixed with a complex array of spices giving them their unique flavour. These kababs are unforgettable when well made and are one of the more favoured ones.

Ingredients

- 500 gms lamb mince
- 3 tbsp raw papaya paste
- 2 tbsp ginger-garlic paste
- A pinch of freshly grated nutmeg
- A few drops of rose essence
- 1 tsp salt
- 3–4 tbsp ghee to fry the kababs

- 1 tsp coriander seeds
- 1 brown cardamom
- 3 green cardamoms
- 4 cloves
- ½" cassia stick
- ¼ tsp cubeb pepper or kabab chini
- A little lichen or patthar ka phool

THE GARAM MASALA

- A few flakes of mace
- ¼ tsp whole black peppercorns
- ½ tsp cumin seeds

Method

1 The essence of these kababs is primarily in their silky, smooth texture and softness. In order to make them melt in the mouth, the first thing to do is to grind the mince to a fine paste. Put the mince in a large, heavy mortar, add a few drops of water and start to bash the mince with a heavy stone pestle.

2 Continue beating the mince, till the fibres are completely broken down and the mince has the consistency of a fine paste. Once the meat is pasty, add a few drops of water and mix it with your hands. Then put it into a bowl and set aside.

3 Now dry-roast all the garam masala ingredients in a small hot frying pan, till they release their lovely natural oils, begin to brown a little and are intensely aromatic. Transfer the spices to a heavy mortar or grinder and grind them, till they transform into a fragrant garam masala. Reserve.

4 Add the raw papaya paste, ginger-garlic paste, nutmeg, rose essence, salt and 3–4 tsp of the ground garam masala to the mince. Mix them gently into the mince with your hands, till you have a fairly loose, liquid mixture. Do not be tempted to over-mix it as the texture could become slightly chewy.

5 Cover the bowl and put it in the refrigerator for a couple of hours. When the mixture is nicely set, remove it from the refrigerator and bring it to room temperature.

6 Heat the ghee in a large frying pan on low heat, till it has a nutty aroma. Roll small quantities of the mince mixture, the size of golf balls, into smooth rounds and add them directly to the hot ghee much the same way as when frying fritters.

7 Gently fry all the delicate galawatis in the hot ghee. Do not remove them from the pan after they are cooked. Let them rest there, so that they do not break, till they are a rich golden brown all over.

8 Lift them out with a slotted spoon. Drain the excess ghee on kitchen paper and serve these ready-to-melt-in-the-mouth, fragrant, exotic kababs with a simple mint chutney.

Dhaniwal Korma

(Kashmiri Mutton Curry with Coriander)

5–6 SERVINGS

This fantastic Kashmiri dish, cooked in curd, aromatic spices and plenty of coriander, has an amazingly delicate flavour. The gravy is richly spiced and intensified by reduction.

Method

THE YAKHNI OR STOCK

1 Wash and trim the meat.

2 To make a delicate yakhni or meat stock, put the meat in a medium-sized pressure cooker along with the salt and enough water to come halfway up the meat. Close the cooker and pressure-cook the meat for 30 minutes on low heat, after the cooker reaches full pressure.

3 As the meat cooks under pressure, it will release all its meaty juices into the water to create a stock, which is then used to make the gravy along with the other ingredients, while cooking the meat to tenderness.

4 Once the meat is cooked, release the pressure of the cooker, strain the stock and reserve it. Set the meat aside.

THE KORMA

5 Put the whisked curd into a bowl and add all the spice powders. Whisk them in, till they dissolve completely and the mixture takes on a lovely yellow-green colour.

6 Heat a deep pan and slowly pour in the curd and spice mixture, whisking it constantly with the free hand to prevent the curd from splitting.

7 Add the salt and continue to stir the curd gently on medium heat. Bring the curd up to a gentle boil and then turn the heat down to a simmer. Cook the curd and spice mixture for about 30 minutes, stirring it gently, till the curd is reduced by a third and is a rich yellow-green in colour. By now the spices should be cooked and the curd wonderfully aromatic.

8 Heat the ghee for tempering in a large metal spoon and add the whole spices. Fry them, till they change colour and are fragrant. Spoon the ghee and whole spices into the curd-based gravy, stirring and mixing everything gently to combine well.

9 Continue reducing the rich curd-and-spice-based gravy, till it's completely concentrated, with a creamy texture and a rich, spicy, yellow colour.

10 Add the cooked pieces of meat, top the gravy with the reserved yakhni and stir gently to combine.

Ingredients

1 kg mixed curry-sized pieces of mutton

1 tsp salt

THE KORMA BASE

750 gms whisked curd

1 tsp turmeric powder

1 tsp dried ginger powder

1 tsp fennel powder

1½ tsp coriander powder

1 tsp cumin powder

A pinch of salt

THE TEMPERING

1 tbsp ghee

5 green cardamoms

2 brown cardamoms

1" cassia stick

4–5 cloves

6 whole black peppercorns

11 Bring the korma up to a boil and then turn the heat down. The curd will split slightly, but that's as it should be—a clotted curd and spice texture.

12 Simmer the korma for another 45 minutes or till the meat is beautifully tender, the gravy intense and concentrated, but still somewhat thin in consistency with a rich, shiny, yellow colour. Most of the curd will reduce and the rich residue of the spices will begin to rise to the surface. Stir everything together a few times.

13 Check for a balance of flavours: the korma should be delicately spiced with the coriander and fennel and the curd-based gravy, rich with the meat stock and spices. By this time, the meat should be tender and aromatic with the delicately spiced, rich, gravy.

14 Serve the korma with hot steamed rice.

Dhabé ka Keema
(Punjabi Mince with Tomato and Spices)
4 SERVINGS

. . . .

Packed with plenty of vegetables and meaty goodness, this is a hearty dhaba-style recipe from the north of India. It's a great dish when there are a large number of hungry people to be fed! The mutton or lamb mince can be substituted by beef or chicken, and as always, the recipe is open to one's own interpretation.

Method

1 To make the base for the mince, heat a medium-sized frying pan and add the oil and butter. When the oil is hot and the butter has melted and is golden, add the whole spices and let them crackle to release their aromas and flavour into the cooking medium.

2 Now add the onion and sauté on medium heat, till it turns light golden brown.

3 Stir in the ginger, garlic and green chillies and sauté them, till lightly coloured.

4 Turn up the heat and add the spice powders. Sauté for a couple of minutes, till they are well toasted and dry. Then add a little water and deglaze the pan of the rich deposits, combining the spices with the aromatics at the same time.

5 Bhuno the aromatic spice base a few times with water, till the masala is homogenous and the oil has risen to the surface.

6 Bung in the chopped capsicums and sauté gently on medium heat, till they have softened a little. Add a few more drops of water and stir a couple of times, to combine all the elements properly.

7 Add the mince to the pan and turn up the heat. Cook the mince in the aromatic base, till it is well mixed and evenly browned.

8 Once the mince has browned and begins to release its juices, add the puréed tomatoes, salt and sugar, to balance the acidity of the tomatoes. Mix well, add a cup of water, cover and simmer the mince for a good 30–45 minutes. Stir the mince occasionally.

9 Uncover the pan and stir everything again. Simmer, till the rich spicy tomato gravy is reduced and the mince has absorbed all its flavours. Allow the mince to thicken, till it is really soft and fluffy.

10 Turn off the heat and squeeze in the lime juice.

Ingredients

500 gms fresh minced mutton or lamb, from the rear leg	1 large onion, chopped fine	¾–1 tsp salt
	¼" ginger, chopped fine	A generous pinch of sugar
THE BASE FOR THE MINCE	6 garlic cloves, chopped fine	Juice of ½ a lime
2–3 tsp refined oil	2 green chillies, chopped fine	**THE GARNISH**
3–4 tbsp butter	½ tsp turmeric powder	2 tbsp chopped fresh coriander leaves
1 bay leaf	1 tsp medium-hot red chilli powder	A pinch of freshly ground garam masala
3 green cardamoms	1 tsp coriander powder	
1 tsp cumin seeds	2 green capsicums, chopped fine	A dollop of butter
4 cloves	3 tomatoes, puréed	

11 Garnish with the coriander leaves and sprinkle in the garam masala, which will heighten the taste as soon as it hits the hot mince.

12 Check for a balance of flavours: the mince should be soft and moist and full of the tomatoes and spices of the thick gravy. The capsicums provide some texture along with the bite of the mince itself. The coriander leaves, lime and garam masala should be value adding to the concentrated meaty taste of the mince.

13 Serve the keema hot with a dollop of butter and hot rotis.

Coorgi Pandi Kari
(Coorgi Pork Curry)
3–4 SERVINGS

This pork curry is one of the best-loved in the Coorg region of Karnataka. It typifies the flavours of Coorg: sweet, smoky pork in a hot, spicy-sour curry, and has a really intense and complex taste.

Method

1 First pressure-cook the pork with the salt and a cup of water for 30 minutes on low heat after the cooker reaches full pressure. Remove from heat, and leave to cool. Open the cooker after the pressure is released.

2 Reserve the pork and stock in the cooker for at least 15 minutes.

THE COORGI MASALA PASTE

3 To make the Coorgi masala paste, dry-roast the whole spices, till they turn almost black.

4 Transfer them to a mortar or grinder and grind to make a fine powder. Set aside.

THE AROMATIC PASTE

5 Char the aromatics, namely, the onions, garlic, ginger, curry leaves and green chillies, in a very hot frying pan, till smoky and slightly blackened in places.

6 Transfer them to a heavy mortar or grinder and add the coriander leaves, oil and salt, which help to break down all the ingredients. Grind to make a smooth paste and set aside.

THE CURRY

7 To create the base of the curry, heat the oil in a deep frying pan and swirl the pan to coat it with the oil. Add the mustard seeds and the curry leaves and let them crackle, till aromatic and fragrant.

8 Now add the aromatic paste and bhuno on medium to high heat, adding a little of the pork stock, till well combined and fried.

9 Add a few tbsp of the ground Coorgi masala paste and bhuno well, using the stock again to mix.

10 Next, sprinkle in the turmeric powder and red chilli powder and continue to bhuno, till the oil rises to the surface and the spices are fully cooked.

11 Add the pork, salt and kaachampuli or tamarind extract. Stir in the sugar or jaggery to balance the sourness and round off the flavours. Fry the pork well on high heat, till well coated with the dark curry base of spices and charred aromatics. Continue to fry, till the pork is well coloured by the spice base.

Ingredients

½ kg pork meat and bone or curry pieces

½ tsp salt

THE COORGI MASALA PASTE

½ tsp fenugreek seeds

1 tsp coriander seeds

1 tsp cumin seeds

1½ tsp whole black peppercorns

THE AROMATIC PASTE

2½ medium-sized onions, halved

7–8 garlic cloves

½" ginger

A handful of curry leaves

6–8 hot Kandhari chillies or small hot green chillies

¼ cup chopped fresh coriander leaves and stems

1 tsp refined oil

½ tsp salt

THE CURRY BASE

1 tbsp refined oil

1 tsp mustard seeds

A handful of curry leaves

½ tsp turmeric powder

1½ tsp hot red chilli powder

½ tsp kaachampuli (local Coorgi date and tamarind concentrate) or 2 tsp tamarind extract (see page 10)

¼ tsp salt

½ tsp sugar or grated jaggery (to balance the sourness of the kaachampuli)

GARNISH

2 tbsp chopped fresh coriander leaves

12 Add 1–2 cups of water, turn the heat down to the barest possible, cover and simmer for around an hour or till the pork is tender.

13 Once the pork is cooked, uncover the pan, turn up the heat and reduce the gravy by a quarter, to concentrate it.

14 Check for a balance of flavours: the curry should be thick, peppery hot and robust, as well as spicy and slightly sour from the kaachampuli.

15 Garnish with the coriander leaves.

16 Serve with steamed rice and a cold beverage.

NOTE: Kaachampuli is a very concentrated extract of dates, tamarind and spices. It is very strong and used in small quantities to add a real tangy kick to a curry. It complements the sweetness of pork perfectly. As a substitute, a concentrated tamarind extract, balanced with some jaggery or sugar can be used.

Bhopali Gosht Korma

(Bhopali Mutton Curry)

6 SERVINGS

Bhopal's cuisine, in Madhya Pradesh, was impacted by several Nawabi influences and hence the food is refined and delicately spiced and a real revelation for those who haven't yet eaten in the city. This curry is a perfect example of the cuisine: wonderfully complex yet delicately balanced with the curd and absolutely delicious.

Ingredients

1 kg mixed pieces of mutton

THE MASALA PASTE

1" ginger

6 garlic cloves

2 medium-sized onions, quartered

1 tsp cumin seeds

1 tsp coriander seeds

¼ tsp whole black peppercorns

Small pieces of mace

A pinch of grated nutmeg

½" cassia stick

6 cloves

3 green cardamoms, seeds only

1 brown cardamom, seeds only

1 bay leaf

A pinch of salt

THE CURRY BASE

2–3 tsp refined oil

1 tsp salt

1½ cups whisked curd

1 tsp turmeric powder

2 tsp medium-hot red chilli powder

GARNISH

¼" ginger, sliced in thin juliennes

3 tbsp chopped fresh coriander leaves

Juice of ½ a lime

Method

1 Clean, trim and wash the meat.

2 Put it in a deep pan with 1 cup of water and the salt. Cover and bring to a boil on high heat. Turn the heat down and simmer the meat while you make the rest of the curry.

3 Boiling the meat will par-cook it and result in a meaty stock or yakhni, which will finally form the medium of the curry. Once the meat is 70 per cent cooked, turn off the heat and leave it to cool in its stock.

THE MASALA PASTE

4 While the meat is simmering, make the masala paste by dry-roasting all the ingredients in a hot frying pan, till they are wonderfully aromatic and have released their natural oils.

5 Transfer them to a heavy mortar or grinder and grind to a fine consistency. Set aside.

THE CURRY

6 Heat a heavy, deep pan and add the oil. When the oil is hot, add the masala paste and sauté it on medium heat using a little water to combine the spices well and bhuno for a few minutes, till the oil surfaces.

7 Now add the cooked meat pieces and fry them gently in the masala base, till they are light brown and fully coated with the masala. Season with salt and mix well.

8 Stir in the whisked curd and the meat stock. Turn the heat down to a simmer, cover and cook the meat for about 45 minutes or till it is perfectly tender and the oil has surfaced, signalling that the curry is properly cooked.

9 It is essential that the curd-based gravy does not boil violently, else it will split. So keep adjusting the temperature while it is on the stove.

10 Check for a balance of flavours: the curry should be delicately meaty and have the combined aroma and taste of all the spices. Further, the meat should be falling off the bone and the curry should be medium-thick in consistency.

11 Serve the korma garnished with thin ginger juliennes, chopped coriander leaves and the lime juice squeezed in to lift all the refined flavours.

12 Serve with hot butter naan.

Kosha Mangsho
(Bengali Mutton Masala)
6 SERVINGS

This mutton recipe is from Bengal and is one of the most robust, refined and perfectly balanced ones that I've ever come across. Amongst other things, what is amazing and unique about Kosha Mangsho is that its thick, coating gravy is fantastically concentrated.

Ingredients

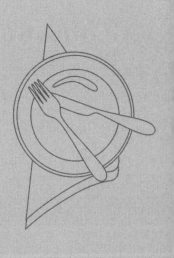

- 1 kg of mixed curry-sized pieces of mutton
- 3 tbsp mustard oil
- 1 tsp cumin seeds
- 4 green cardamoms
- 4 cloves
- ½" cassia stick
- 2 onions, grated fine
- 3 tsp ginger-garlic paste
- 1 tsp medium-hot red chilli powder
- ½ tsp turmeric powder
- ½ tsp sugar
- 2 cups hung curd
- 1 tsp salt

Method

1 Wash and trim the meat. Set aside.

2 Heat the mustard oil in a deep, heavy pan on high heat, till it smokes, to burn off its bitterness.

3 When the oil is almost clear in colour, turn the heat down and add the whole spices to the pan. Fry the spices for a few minutes to release their aromas and flavour the oil delicately.

4 Now add the grated onions and sauté on medium heat, till golden brown. Add the ginger-garlic paste and sauté for a few minutes longer.

5 Stir in the spice powders and sauté for a couple of minutes to toast the spices. Add a little water to deglaze the pan and bhuno repeatedly with water, till the base is homogenous and rich brown.

6 When the oil rises to the surface and the spices are cooked, add 4–5 pieces of meat at a time and fry them in the aromatic spice base on high heat, till the meat is richly brown and coated with the masala. Add the sugar and continue to fry to further caramelize the meat and masala.

7 Sprinkle in a little water and deglaze the pan to pick up those rich pan deposits. Mix well and turn the heat down to medium-low.

8 Gently mix in the hung curd and stir, till it coats the meat properly.

9 Season with salt and cover the pan. Simmer the meat on the lowest possible heat for 1½ hours or till it is tender and the gravy coating it is really thick.

10 Once the meat is tender, uncover the pan to reduce the gravy a little. Mix well to coat the meat in the gravy again and scrape up any pan deposits into the thick gravy.

11 Check for a balance of flavours: the gravy should be aromatic and delicately spiced with the whole spices and mildly tart with the hung curd. The meat should be extremely tender and packed with the delicate character of the thick masala gravy, with the robustness of the mustard oil coming through.

12 Serve with steamed rice.

Kolhapuri Mutton Chops

4–6 SERVINGS

. . . .

The people of Kolhapur, Maharashtra, are known to love mutton, and indeed, this is one of the best preparations from across the country. This particular dish brings together the flavours of the region: it's not only bold and robust but intensely spicy and meaty.

Method

1 Wash and trim the chops. Drain thoroughly.

2 Combine the marinade ingredients in a bowl and mix in the chops. Cover and refrigerate for an hour or so.

3 Grind the garam masala ingredients in a mortar or grinder. Set aside.

4 To make the Kohlapuri masala paste, heat the oil in a medium-sized frying pan and fry the julienned onions, till they are dark brown and crisp.

5 Take them off the heat, transfer to a plate and leave them to cool. Reserve the oil.

6 While the onions are left to cool, transfer 2 tbsp of the reserved oil to a hot frying pan. Swirl the pan to coat the base and sear the chops in batches of 4, till they are well browned, with a rich caramelized crust. Season them with salt and remove to a bowl along with all the pan juices. Cover and set aside.

7 Put the fried onions into a heavy mortar or grinder along with the grated coconut, ginger, garlic, salt and a few drops of water. Grind them into a semi-fine paste. Set aside.

THE CURRY

8 Heat a deep sauté pan. Add 2 tsp of the onion-flavoured oil and swirl the pan to coat the base. Add the finely chopped onion and sauté on medium heat for a few minutes, till soft but not coloured.

9 Add the ground Kolhapuri masala paste and bhuno it with a little water.

10 Mix in the spice powders and continue to bhuno on high heat, till well roasted. Continue to bhuno the aromatic and spice base adding a little water to prevent it from burning and to deglaze the pan.

11 After the base becomes homogenous, add the tomatoes and bhuno again, till they are fully cooked and completely amalgamated with the other ingredients.

12 Now the base is ready. Add the chops and fry them in the base for a few minute to coat well.

Ingredients

1 kg tender mutton chops	**THE KOLHAPURI MASALA PASTE**	1 tsp hot red chilli powder
½ tsp salt	1 cup refined oil	½ tsp cumin powder
THE MARINADE	1 cup finely julienned onions	1 tsp coriander powder
1 level tsp turmeric powder	½ cup grated dried coconut	3 tomatoes, chopped fine
1 tsp red chilli powder	¾" ginger	2 tbsp chopped coriander leaves
2 tsp refined oil	6 garlic cloves	Juice of ½ a lime
THE GARAM MASALA	A pinch of salt to help grind the ingredients	
1/8" cassia stick	**THE CURRY BASE**	
1/6 tsp grated nutmeg	1 onion, chopped fine	
3 green cardamoms	1 tsp turmeric powder	
½ brown cardamom		

13 Sprinkle in a few drops of water, cover the pan and turn the heat down. Let the chops simmer gently for 25–30 minutes or till they are succulent, tender and bursting with the flavours of the masala.

14 Uncover the pan to reduce the gravy for a few minutes.

15 Stir in the ground garam masala powder and coriander leaves and squeeze in the lime juice.

16 Check for seasoning and a balance of flavours: the gravy should be a thick, clinging masala. It should be robust, spicy and sweet with a distinct taste of tomatoes. Ensure that the chops are well coated with the curry base.

17 Rest the chops for 5–7 minutes before serving.

18 Serve with a traditional rice bhakri or hot roti.

Ladakhi Mutton Thukpa
(Ladakhi Meat and Vegetable Broth)
5–6 SERVINGS

. . . .

This is the kind of cooking I have always loved. The clean delicate flavours—hearty and nourishing with perfectly cooked root vegetables, meltingly tender meat and a great tasting broth. It can be served with a variety of different toppings to create different combinations as well.

The Chakh le India Cookbook

Method

1 Wash and trim the meat of excess fat.

2 Next, sear the meat. Heat a deep sauté pan. Add the oil and swirl the pan to coat it. When the oil is hot, season the meat well with salt and some freshly ground pepper. Sear the meat in batches on all sides, making sure they aren't moved around too much. This ensures that they develop a rich caramelized brown crust all over.

3 After all the meat pieces are a rich, light brown, add the onions, ginger and garlic. Sauté on medium heat, till they are soft but not coloured, and the pan is wonderfully aromatic. Add 2 litres of water and deglaze the pan well, scraping up the rich pan deposits. The water is added to form the soup for the thukpa.

4 Sprinkle in the salt and the whole peppercorns and stir well to combine. Cover the pan, turn the heat down to low and simmer the meat and aromatics for about 45 minutes or so, till the meat is 70 per cent cooked (see note).

5 Uncover the pan and add the carrots, radish and coriander leaves.

6 Stir well, cover the pan and simmer on low heat for another 45 minutes or till the vegetables are cooked but still firm and the meat is tender. The thukpa will have a fantastic aroma from the coriander leaves, vegetables and meat.

7 Reduce the stock for the last 10 minutes on medium heat.

8 Check for a balance of flavours: the thukpa should be delicately meaty and carry all the lovely flavours of the vegetables, aromatics and herbs.

9 Add the egg noodles and simmer gently for about 6–8 minutes, depending on the thickness of the noodles, till they are cooked but not mushy. Stir the thukpa one last time and squeeze some lime juice to give it a good citrus tang.

10 Turn off the heat and leave it to mature for a few minutes.

11 Serve the thukpa with any or all of the toppings handed around separately.

Ingredients

- 1 kg lamb shanks or leg and shoulder chunks
- 3 tsp refined oil
- 1 tsp salt
- ½ tsp freshly ground black pepper
- 2 onions, cut into thick juliennes
- 1" ginger, sliced into thin strips
- 6–8 garlic cloves, kept whole
- ½ tsp salt
- ½ tsp whole black peppercorns
- 2 carrots, sliced into long, slender pieces
- 1 daikon radish or white radish, sliced into slender pieces
- ½ cup chopped fresh coriander leaves and stems
- 200 gms fresh dried egg noodles, broken in half
- Juice of 1–2 limes

TOPPINGS

- Hot chilli oil
- Sweet chilly sauce
- Soy sauce
- Deep-fried chopped garlic
- Fried onion slices
- Dried red chillies, broken
- Hard-boiled eggs, sliced
- Spring onions, sliced in fine rings
- Peanuts
- Chopped fresh coriander leaves
- Lime wedges

NOTE: Gently skim the albumen and impurities that rise to the surface as the meat simmers. Use a tablespoon or serving ladle to gently skim off the surface of the broth for a clear, tasty broth. Bring the broth to a boil only after most of the scum has been removed.

Mutton Seekh Kabab
(Minced Mutton Kabab)

4 SERVINGS

. . . .

Seekh kababs are commonly found all over the world in several different guises. In India too, there is a large variety of skewered mince kababs. It's a great appetizer or starter for a party or can be stuffed into a parantha with some salad for an instant seekh roll meal.

Ingredients

500 gms mutton mince	Juice of ½ a lime
100 gms lamb kidney fat, minced	**TO COOK THE KABABS**
2 tbsp ginger-garlic paste	6 square metal skewers
1 tsp turmeric powder	2–3 tsp butter
1 tsp red chilli powder	**THE GARNISH**
½ tsp cumin powder	1 onion, sliced in rings
1 tsp coriander powder	6 lime wedges
A few fresh coriander leaves	2 tbsp chopped fresh coriander leaves
A few fresh mint leaves	
1 tsp salt	
2 tsp refined oil	

Method

1 Squeeze out the excess moisture from the mince and put it into a bowl. Add the kidney fat, ginger-garlic paste, spice powders, herbs, salt and oil and knead it gently with your hands.

2 Ensure that all the ingredients are evenly mixed and well blended. The kidney fat is imperative in making good seekh kababs, as it keeps the mixture moist and succulent when cooked, while helping the mix to bind.

3 Once the mix is sticky and pliable, cover the bowl and put it in the refrigerator to rest and firm up for about an hour or so.

4 Heat a grill, till hot or preheat an oven to 180ºC.

5 Remove the mixture from the refrigerator. Use a little water to wet your hands and palms as it will help in handling the sticky mince while also smoothing out the kabab as it is formed around the skewer.

6 Take a small fist-sized portion of the mixture in your left palm and place a skewer in the centre of the mix. Gently wrap the mixture around the skewer, carefully stretching it further up and all around to make an 8" long kabab. Repeat the process, till 6 nice smooth kababs are ready for the grill.

TO COOK THE KABABS

7 To grill the kababs, baste them with a little melted butter and grill them 3"– 4" away from the heat or roast them suspended in a roasting tray in the preheated oven. Turn the kababs a few times to ensure even cooking, till the internal fat is sizzling, the kababs are a lovely caramelized golden brown and the meat is cooked through perfectly.

8 When all the kababs are golden and juicy, carefully remove them from the skewers with the help of a clean cloth. Arrange them on a platter and squeeze some lime juice over them.

9 Next garnish them with the onion rings, lime wedges and coriander leaves and serve the succulent seekh kababs straight away with a mint chutney.

Dhaniwal Korma
Pg 14

Kosha Mangsho
Pg 21

Dhabé ka Keema
Pg 16

Bheja Masala
Pg 34

Mutton Yakhni

(Kashmiri Mutton in Curd and Aromatic Spices)

6 SERVINGS

. . . .

There are very few dishes that can match the delicate and amazing flavour of a great mutton yakhni. It's a technique that can only be defined as pure genius. Although it is fairly simple to do, the results are spectacular. All one needs is a little care and patience to produce one of the best mutton dishes ever. You have to try it!

Ingredients

1 kg mutton chest and rib pieces
1 tsp salt

THE GRAVY

750 gms well-whisked curd
3 brown cardamoms
4–5 green cardamoms
3–4 cloves
1" cassia stick
2 tsp dried ginger powder
3 tbsp aniseed powder
3–4 tbsp dried mint leaves

Method

1 Wash and trim the meat.

2 Then, pressure-cook it with 1¼ cups of water and the salt for about 30 minutes on low heat, after the cooker reaches full pressure, till the meat is about 80 per cent cooked. The meat juices and the water create a tasty stock which finally provides the real flavour to the finished dish.

3 Reserve the meat and the stock and set aside.

THE GRAVY

4 To make the curd-based gravy, heat a deep pan, add the curd and stir continuously with a balloon whisk or wooden spoon on low to medium heat, to prevent the curd from splitting.

5 Once the curd has the consistency of milk, add the whole spices and continue stirring for about 10 minutes or till the curd is infused with the spices.

6 Add the dried ginger powder and cook for a few minutes longer.

7 Stir in the aniseed powder and combine well. By now, the gravy should be delicately aromatic with the aniseed, ginger and whole spices. Continue stirring for a few minutes longer.

8 Add the meat along with its stock and stir gently to blend well.

9 Check for seasoning and add a little salt if needed.

10 Add the mint leaves and stir well. Cook for another 20 minutes, on a very low simmer, stirring gently all the while.

11 Check for a balance of flavours: the yakhni should be slightly meaty, with the meat falling off the bone and amazingly aromatic from the delicate spices and the mint. It should also be slightly sour, with the curd and meat stock perfectly blended.

12 Cover and keep for 3–4 hours to let the yakhni mature. Then heat through and serve with hot steamed rice and a Kashmiri onion chutney.

Rogan Josh
(Kashmiri Mutton)

5–6 SERVINGS

One of Kashmir's most popular meat dishes, this robust, spicy and intensely flavoured curry is incredible when made correctly. The entire recipe is based on the technique of repeated, frying/sautéing or bhunoing, which creates rich pan juices that form the basis of the meaty, spicy, red gravy or rogan—the deep red oil and fats that rise to the surface of the dish.

Method

1 Wash and trim the meat.

THE KASHMIRI GARAM MASALA

2 To make the fresh garam masala, dry-roast the whole spices on medium heat, till they are aromatic. Transfer them to a heavy mortar or grinder. Grind them to make a fine powder and set aside.

THE CURRY

3 Put the mustard oil in a heavy kadhai or deep pan on high heat till it smokes, to burn off its bitterness. When the oil is almost clear in colour, take it off the heat and leave to cool for a few minutes.

4 Once cooled, put the pan back on medium heat and then add the cassia, cloves and cardamoms. Sauté them, till they begin to change colour and are crackling and aromatic.

5 Add the meat, turn up the heat and sear it on all sides in the hot oil, till it turns a rich, golden brown and mustard-yellow in colour.

6 Add the sugar and continue frying, till the meat is richly caramelized and golden brown and the oil rises to the surface.

7 Stir in the spice powders and salt and continue to bhuno the meat, creating a deep red, intense and rich caramel in the base of the pan. If the spices begin to smell burnt or singed, add a few drops of water and deglaze the pan juices at the bottom of the pan. The meat will be a deep reddish brown and the pan will be rather dry.

8 Add the chopped tomatoes now and continue to bhuno, using the moisture in the tomatoes to deglaze the rich pan deposits on the base.

9 Continue to fry, till the tomatoes disintegrate fully and are almost completely absorbed by the meat, turning the rich thick masala even richer in the process.

10 Stir in the whisked curd. Fry on medium heat, till the curd is fully absorbed by the meat and spices in the pan and the thick masala is even richer in colour and slightly creamy in texture.

11 After the curd is absorbed, add 2 cups of water, scraping up all the coagulated pan juices on the base of the pan. Bring everything to a boil on high heat, to amalgamate the flavours.

Ingredients

1 kg mixed curry-sized pieces of mutton	**THE CURRY BASE**	1 tsp salt
	5 tbsp mustard oil	1 ripe tomato, chopped fine
THE KASHMIRI GARAM MASALA	½" cassia stick	1 cup whisked curd
1 brown cardamom	4 cloves	
4 green cardamoms	1 brown cardamom	
½" cassia stick	3 green cardamoms	
4 cloves	1 tsp sugar	
1½ tsp cumin seeds	1½ tsp red Kashmiri chilli powder	
1 tsp coriander seeds	1 tsp fennel powder	
¼ tsp whole black peppercorns	1 tsp dried ginger powder	

12 Turn the heat down, cover the pan and simmer the meat for 1½–2 hours, or till the meat is fork tender and there is a layer of deep red oil floating on the surface of the gravy. This red oil is the rogan mentioned above and is the result of the constant and lengthy bhunoing of the meat, spices and curd in the hot mustard oil.

13 Taste and add more salt if required.

14 Simmer the curry for 15–20 minutes uncovered, to reduce and concentrate it further and then sprinkle 1 tsp of the ground garam masala.

15 As soon as the spice powder hits the simmering curry, it will explode with aroma and taste. Stir it in.

16 Check for a balance of flavours: the meat should be tender, succulent and infused with all the flavours of the spices, curd, tomatoes and mustard oil. The brilliantly red gravy should be intensely spicy, aromatic and meaty, with the garam masala giving it an exotic and delicately aromatic character on the finish.

17 Serve with hot steamed rice.

Banjara Maas
(Banjara-style Mutton)
6 SERVINGS

. . . .

The Banjara or nomadic tribes of Rajasthan are known for their butch and robust cuisine. The mustard oil and dried red chillies give this dish a distinct flavour and the garam masala lends a lovely aromatic finish to the mutton.

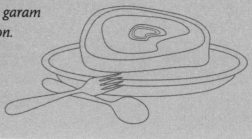

Method

1 Wash the meat and trim it. Cut it into pieces and set aside.

THE GARAM MASALA POWDER

2 Dry-roast all the whole spices and bay leaf in a small frying pan on low to medium heat, till they release their aroma. Transfer to a heavy mortar or grinder and grind to make a fine powder which should also have an intense, aromatic fragrance. Set aside.

THE CURRY

3 Heat the mustard oil in a deep, heavy pan on high heat till it smokes, to burn off its bitterness.

4 Now, add the onions and sauté on medium to high heat, till they begin to colour lightly.

5 Add the red chillies and sauté, till crisp.

6 Next, mix in the ginger-garlic paste and sauté on high heat, till it begins to turn light brown.

7 Stir in the spice powders and mix well. Sprinkle in a little water and thoroughly deglaze the pan, to pick up the rich deposits on its base. Sauté well, adding a little water at a time, and bhuno repeatedly, till the oil begins to surface and the spices are fully cooked. The aromatic spice base will be a rich brown.

8 Add the meat and season with salt. Fry the meat, till it is a rich golden brown.

9 Mix in the sugar and continue frying the meat, till it is well coated by the masala and richly browned and caramelized.

10 The meat will begin to release its juices. Use these to deglaze the pan periodically, the rich masala and meat juices forming a rich, thick gravy.

11 Turn the heat down and add the whisked curd. Mix it in well, till the curd begins to dry up and is absorbed by the meat.

The Chakh le India Cookbook

Ingredients

1 kg mutton, shoulder, ribs and leg	**THE CURRY BASE**	½ tsp sugar
THE GARAM MASALA POWDER	3–4 tbsp mustard oil	1 cup whisked curd
Small pieces of mace	2 onions, julienned	Juice of ½ a lime
½ tsp cumin seeds	3–4 hot dried red chillies	**THE TEMPERING**
1 brown cardamom	3 tsp ginger-garlic paste	½ tsp cracked coriander seeds
2 green cardamoms	1 tsp turmeric powder	
¼" cassia stick	1 tsp hot red chilli powder	
3 cloves	2 tsp coriander powder	
½ a bay leaf	1 tsp salt	

12 Cover the pan and simmer for about an hour or till the meat is tender and the gravy is thick. Uncover the pan and simmer on medium heat to reduce and concentrate the gravy further.

13 Sprinkle the ground garam masala powder over the dish and mix well to combine.

14 Add the cracked coriander seeds and mix it into the thick masala gravy. Simmer for a couple of minutes more and turn off the heat.

15 Check for a balance of flavours: the gravy should be thick and spicy, blending well with the creamy sourness of the curd. The meat should be perfectly tender and bursting with the rich concentrated flavours of the gravy.

16 Squeeze in the lime juice and serve with hot tandoori roti.

Bheja Masala

(Masala Brain)

When cooking lambs' or goats' brain, it's important to take into account its delicate, almost buttery flavour. This recipe brings that out perfectly while infusing the brain with plenty of aroma. A must cook if you haven't tried cooking brains before. Creamy and delicious!

Method

1 First, gently boil the brains with the salt. Put them into a frying pan and add enough water to cover and bring it to a boil. Turn the heat down and simmer the brains, till soft and cooked through. The impurities will rise to the top; skim them off with a spoon.

2 After the brains have simmered for about 10 minutes and most of the impurities have been skimmed, remove the soft, cooked brains from the water and drain in a sieve. Carefully remove any pieces of grit or impurities that may be clinging to them. Set aside.

THE CURRY

3 To make the base for the dish, heat the oil in a hot frying pan. Add the green chilli and toss it for a few seconds. Then add the cumin seeds and cassia and sauté, till they are crackling and aromatic.

4 Add the onion and sauté on medium heat, till they are a light golden.

5 Stir in the ginger and garlic and continue to sauté, till they are soft and fragrant.

6 Sprinkle in the spice powders and sauté, till they are fragrant and well toasted.

7 Turn up the heat and add a little water to deglaze the pan and lift all the pan deposits on the base. Bhuno the masala a few times with water, till they are fully combined and the oil rises to the surface.

8 Add the salt and the chopped tomatoes and fry on medium heat, till the tomatoes begin to disintegrate slightly. In order to make the tomatoes softer, add a little water and bhuno for a few minutes longer. The oil will rise to the surface, which means the spices are fully cooked and the base is ready with a rich, reddish-yellow colour.

9 Gently immerse the par-cooked brains and gently scramble them like eggs, using a fork. Toss the brains in the masala, till they are well coated with the spices. Turn the heat to a simmer, cover the pan and cook the brains for 10–12 minutes.

10 When the brains are soft and fluffy, rather like oozy scrambled eggs in texture, uncover the pan and

Ingredients

3 lambs' or goats' brains	½ tsp turmeric powder
½ tsp salt	½ tsp medium-hot red chilli powder
THE CURRY BASE	1 tsp coriander powder
3 tsp refined oil	1 tsp salt
1 green chilli, slit	2 tomatoes, chopped fine
½ tsp cumin seeds	Juice of ½ a lime
¼" cassia stick	3 tbsp chopped fresh coriander leaves
1 onion, chopped fine	A knob of butter
¼" ginger, chopped fine	
5 garlic cloves, chopped fine	

stir everything a few times to combine them well. Don't be tempted to cook the brains any longer as they will dry out and become rubbery.

11 Turn off the heat and toss the ingredients a couple of times to make sure the brain and the aromatic spice base are fully combined. Squeeze in the lime juice to provide a citrus tang, sprinkle some coriander leaves and add a knob of butter, gently folding it in.

12 Check for a balance of flavours: the brains should be delicately meaty, soft, fluffy and creamy in texture with the simple spices of the base just serving to accentuate their delicate flavour without overpowering them. The butter gives the dish a lovely, silky, buttery finish with the lime lifting the dish perfectly.

13 Serve the brains hot with hot roti.

Punjabi Mutton Chops

4–6 SERVINGS

This fantastic recipe for meaty lamb chops uses a typical Punjabi marinade, with plenty of onions, tomatoes and herbs. Spicy and delicious, it's a genuine kadhai-style recipe that can be made with a variety of meats.

Ingredients

1 kg slightly fatty mutton chops

2 tsp refined oil

THE MARINADE

½" ginger

6 garlic cloves

4 hot green chillies

½ tsp cumin seeds

½" cassia stick

1 tsp coriander seeds

½ tsp turmeric powder

½ tsp hot red chilli powder

½–¾ tsp salt

2 tsp malt vinegar

THE KHADA MASALA

½ tsp cumin seeds

2 medium-sized onions, julienned

2 tomatoes, sliced into long strips

2 green chillies, slit

Juice of 1 lime

1 cup chopped fresh coriander leaves

Method

1 Wash and trim the chops off sinew and gristle.

2 Next, to marinate the chops, dry-roast the ginger, garlic, green chillies and whole spices in a hot pan, till aromatic. Transfer them to a mortar or grinder and add the spice powders, salt and vinegar. Grind to make a fine paste.

3 Put the chops into a bowl and add the marinade paste to it. Rub the paste into the chops with your hands. Cover and leave to marinate in the refrigerator for about 30 minutes.

4 To cook the chops, remove them from the refrigerator and bring them to room temperature.

5 Heat a frying pan, add the oil and swirl the pan to coat it well. When hot, add the chops in batches and sear them on both sides on medium to high heat, till browned with a rich caramelized crust.

6 Return all the seared chops to the pan and fry on medium heat for a few minutes. Add a little water and deglaze the rich pan deposits.

7 Fry, till all the water evaporates and the oil begins to separate.

8 Now add the cumin seeds and the julienned onions and sauté on medium heat, till they are a light golden brown.

9 Add the tomatoes and green chillies, turn up the heat and fry everything together for a couple of minutes, stirring vigorously to combine well.

10 Once the tomatoes have softened a little, add a cup or so of water and deglaze the pan again. Bring to a gentle boil, turn the heat down and simmer for 8–10 minutes or till the tomatoes begin to disintegrate slightly, the masala gravy is thick and the chops are tender and succulent.

11 Squeeze in the lime juice and sprinkle the coriander leaves.

12 Check for a balance of flavours: the gravy should be thick, richly spiced and tangy, and should coat the chops well. The meat should be really tenderand juicy with the rich tomato-based khada masala gravy.

13 Serve warm with hot roti or parantha and a tangy onion salad.

Chicken
RECIPES

Achari Murgh Kabab
Pg 40

Sailana Junglee Murgh
(Sailana Chicken)

Sailana cuisine is from the Marwar region in Rajasthan. It is one of the most exotic in the country and must have been cooked with game meat in the early days but chicken works well with this recipe. A perfect example of how a few simple ingredients can be transformed into the most delicate and fantastic dish. This one is strictly for special occasions and is undoubtedly one of the most incredible chicken recipes.

Ingredients

1 chicken without skin

1 tsp salt

8–10 hot dried red chillies, soaked in warm water for 30 minutes

8–10 garlic cloves, sliced lengthwise in half

500 gms ghee

Method

1 Cut the chicken into 8 large pieces—legs, thighs and breast pieces—and trim them. Wash well, drain and dry with kitchen towels.

2 Take a deep-sided pan or one that is large enough to hold the chicken in a single layer. Add the chicken pieces, salt, soaked and drained red chillies and garlic. Add enough ghee to submerge the chicken almost fully.

3 Turn on the heat to a fairly low simmer, cover and gently poach the chicken in the hot ghee for about 15 minutes. Make sure the pieces are fully submerged in ghee. Now turn the heat down to the barest possible simmer and continue poaching the chicken, covered, for another 1½ hours or till it is tender.

4 Check for seasoning and add some more salt if required. By now the garlic and chillies should be super soft and the ghee, wonderfully aromatic and light red.

5 Check for a balance of flavours: the chicken should be almost coming off the bone and really succulent and tasty. The ghee should be robust and slightly spicy with the chillies and garlic.

6 If possible, leave the pan in a warm place for a couple of hours to let the curry mature.

7 Serve with steamed rice.

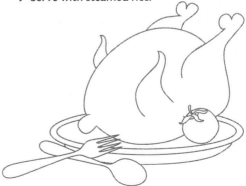

Achari Murgh Kabab
(Pickled Chicken Kabab)

6 SERVINGS

. . . .

These robust, pickle-style, spicy, tangy, marinated chicken kababs are easy to make. They can be marinated just a few hours before they are to be served and later grilled to succulent perfection.

Method

1 Cut the chicken into medium-sized pieces: 2 drumsticks, 2 thighs, 4 breast pieces and wings. Wash the chicken thoroughly and dry it on kitchen paper. Make sure the skin covers the flesh well. Make a few gashes on each of the pieces to help the marinade penetrate the meat and set aside.

THE ACHARI MARINADE

2 To make the sour and spicy pickle-style marinade, put the mustard oil in a small frying pan on high heat, till it smokes, but is still quite yellow and pungent in aroma.

3 Add all the marinade ingredients except the lime juice and fry them in the hot oil, till they crackle and are intensely aromatic. Ensure that the garlic and ginger turn a nice, light golden brown.

4 Turn off the heat and transfer the ingredients to a heavy mortar or grinder. Grind to make a deep, yellowy-golden paste that's fairly coarse in consistency. Mix the paste well with a spoon and reserve.

5 Put the chicken pieces into a large non-reactive bowl and add the pungent marinade. Squeeze in the lime juice and then massage the rich, fiery hot paste into the chicken, making sure that the pieces are coated evenly. Cover and put into the refrigerator to marinate for 2–4 hours. Turn the pieces in the marinade halfway through to ensure that the chicken marinates evenly.

6 Once the chicken is marinated, remove it from the refrigerator and bring it to room temperature.

TO COOK AND SERVE THE KABABS

7 Preheat the grill, till it is searing hot, or an oven's broiler. (The chicken can also be drizzled with some oil or butter and roasted in the oven.)

8 Once the grill is hot, season the chicken well with salt, and sear the pieces on the hottest part of the grill, till they are golden and charred on the first side. Turn the pieces over carefully using tongs and sear them on the second side to give them a crisp caramelized crust.

9 Turn the heat down and gently grill the pieces, basting them with the melted butter and oil, to keep them moist and crisp on the outside. Prick

Ingredients

1 chicken with skin	½ tsp nigella seeds
½ tsp salt	½ tsp turmeric powder
3 tsp melted butter	1 tsp red chilli powder
2 tsp oil	3 hot green chillies
THE ACHARI MARINADE	¼ tsp freshly ground white pepper
2 tbsp mustard oil	A few curry leaves
6 garlic cloves	½ tsp salt
½" ginger	Juice of 1½ limes
1 tsp coriander seeds	**TO SERVE**
½ tsp cumin seeds	Juice of ½ a lime
½ tsp fennel seeds	

the flesh with a fork to ensure that the chicken is firm and the juices run clear.

10 The chicken can also be tested for its firmness and fully cooked condition using a meat thermometer. Grill the chicken till it reads 180°F.

11 When the chicken is crisp and golden and cooked to perfection, take the pieces off the heat and put them on a platter to rest and absorb their juices.

12 Squeeze some lime juice on them for a delicious citrus twist and serve these robust, spicy, tangy, charred, grilled chicken kababs straight away.

dhra Chicken Lollipops

5 SERVINGS

A deliciously spicy and tangy dish from Andhra Pradesh, it is perfect as a heavy snack for a cocktail party or as an appetizer before the main course. As the name suggests, this recipe is cooked with crisp, golden brown, chicken lollipops in a hot, thick, dry Andhra masala, but can also be made with prawns, fish, beef or any other ingredient for equally amazing results.

Method

1 Wash the lollipops and dry them on kitchen paper.

THE MARINADE

2 Combine the marinade ingredients in a small bowl. Put the lollipops into another bowl and rub the marinade into them with your hands. Cover and set aside.

THE HOT ANDHRA MASALA PASTE

3 To make the masala paste, put a small frying pan on medium heat. When hot, add the oil. Once the oil is hot, add all the masala paste ingredients, starting with the red chillies and ending with the turmeric powder. Fry them, till they release their natural oils and are wonderfully crisp and aromatic.

4 Next, transfer them to a heavy mortar or grinder with the salt. Add a little water and grind the spices, till the paste is of a fine consistency. Keep it aside.

TO SEAR THE LOLLIPOPS

5 Now, heat a medium-sized frying pan and add a tsp of oil. Once hot, add the marinated lollipops to the pan and sear them in two batches, till they are a lovely golden brown. Transfer the seared lollipops to a plate and keep them warm.

THE CURRY

6 To make the base, heat 3 tsp of oil in the same pan used to sear the lollipops and add the mustard seeds, fenugreek seeds and curry leaves. Sauté them for a few minutes, till they are crackling and really nutty.

7 Throw in the shallots and sauté, till they are soft.

8 Mix in the hot masala paste and sauté on medium to high heat for a couple of minutes. Sprinkle in a few drops of water and bhuno the paste repeatedly, till it's a rich, dark reddish colour and the oil rises to the surface.

9 Add the tamarind extract and the jaggery and stir to combine them well. Sauté the paste for a few minutes longer, adding a little water if it appears too dry. Season with salt and mix. The base for the lollipops is now ready.

10 Turn up the heat to high and add the seared lollipops along with their resting juices. Fry the lollipops in the hot, spicy and aromatic base, till they are well coated with the masala and are a rich, deep, dark brown.

Ingredients

10 chicken lollipops	4 hot green chillies	½ tsp mustard seeds
1 tsp refined oil	1 tsp cumin seeds	½ tsp fenugreek seeds
THE MARINADE	1 tsp coriander seeds	A few curry leaves
½ tsp turmeric powder	1 tsp fennel seeds	5–6 shallots, julienned
½ tsp red chilli powder	½ tsp whole black peppercorns	3 tbsp thick tamarind extract (see page 10)
½ tsp salt	½" cassia stick	1–2 tsp grated jaggery, to balance
1 tsp refined oil	4–5 cloves	¼ tsp salt
THE HOT ANDHRA MASALA PASTE	A few curry leaves	**TO SERVE**
2–3 tsp refined oil	¼ bunch of fresh coriander leaves	Juice of ½ a lime
6–8 hot dried red Guntur chillies	½ tsp turmeric powder	2–3 tsp chopped fresh coriander leaves
6–8 dried red bor chillies	½ tsp salt	
¾" ginger	**THE CURRY BASE**	
6–8 garlic cloves	3 tsp refined oil	

11 Turn the heat down, add a few drops of water to deglaze the pan and stir everything together. Cover the pan and cook the lollipops on medium heat, till they are perfectly tender.

12 Uncover the pan and reduce the thick coating masala for a few minutes to make it intensely spicy and tangy. Once the oil has surfaced and the masala is thick and glossy, turn off the heat.

13 Check for a balance of flavours: the lollipops should be tender and bursting with the intensely spicy and tangy coating of the Andhra masala that's perfectly balanced with the tamarind, jaggery and spices. The curry leaves and mustard seeds provide the quint-essential nuttiness that is so characteristic of South Indian cuisines.

14 Serve the lollipops hot with a squeeze of lime juice and some coriander leaves sprinkled over them and enjoy them with a chilled beer.

Awadhi Biryani

6 SERVINGS

....

The Awadhi biryani is one of the more refined versions of this popular Indian dish. Complex spices, fried onions, curd and plenty of fresh herbs give it a delicate yet special character. It can be cooked to perfection with mutton or lamb. The Awadhi biryani does take some patience, but it's well worth the effort, and is perfect for any occasion.

Method

THE MARINADE

1 Cut the chicken into curry-sized pieces, trim the pieces and wash well. Set aside in a colander to drain thoroughly.

2 To marinate the chicken, heat a medium-sized frying pan and add the oil. Once the oil is hot, add the onions and fry them on medium to high heat, till they turn a deep, rich, dark brown. Remove them with a slotted spoon and spread out on kitchen paper to dry; they will turn crisp once totally dried. Reserve the oil.

3 Now, dry-roast the whole spices and bay leaf and transfer them to a heavy mortar or grinder. Grind to make a fine, aromatic powder.

4 Put the curd, ginger-garlic paste, turmeric powder, chilli powder, the freshly ground garam masala and half the fried onions into a glass bowl. Mix well and add the chicken. Massage the marinade thoroughly into the chicken with your hands.

5 Cover and put into the refrigerator to marinate for 4–6 hours.

THE RICE

6 Wash the rice in several changes of water to remove most of its starch. Soak it in water for 15 minutes.

7 Boil approximately 4 litres of water in a deep pan and add the whole spices. Bring to a boil again and add the salt. Drain the rice and add it to the pan. Cook, till the rice is 80 per cent done and a bit chalky in the centre.

8 Drain the excess water and spread the rice on a platter to cool. At this point, the rice will smell fantastic with the delicate aroma of the spices and the basmati.

THE CHICKEN

9 Remove the marinated chicken from the refrigerator and bring to room temperature. Season with salt and mix well.

10 Now, heat a deep, heavy handi or braising dish and add 2 tbsp of the reserved onion-flavoured oil.

11 Once hot, drain the excess marinade from the chicken, add it to the oil in batches and fry on high heat, till the pieces are light golden brown. Add the leftover marinade, turn the heat down slightly and fry the chicken in its marinade to create a rich, concentrated gravy.

12 Cook the chicken, till it's half done and turn off the heat.

13 (It's essential to a biryani that the gravy of the meat or chicken is reduced and concentrated. When the

Ingredients

1 chicken, without skin	½ tsp black cumin seeds	3 green cardamoms
1 tsp salt	1 bay leaf	4 cloves
2 cups wholewheat flour for the sealing dough	1 cup whisked curd	6 whole black peppercorns
	2–3 tsp ginger-garlic paste	1 tsp salt

THE MARINADE

- 1 cup refined oil
- 3 medium-sized onions, julienned fine
- ½" cassia stick
- 5 cloves
- 1 brown cardamom
- 3 green cardamoms

- ½ tsp turmeric powder
- 1 tsp hot red chilli powder

THE RICE

- 500 gms top quality basmati rice
- ½" cassia stick
- 1 brown cardamom

TO LAYER THE BIRYANI

- ¼ cup fresh coriander leaves
- ½ cup milk
- A few saffron strands
- A dollop of butter

rice is mixed with the chicken, it should flavour the biryani but be dry; not wet.)

14 Turn off the heat and mix the chicken well to coat it in the thick marinade-based masala gravy.

TO LAYER THE BIRYANI

15 To layer the biryani, take the handi or clay pot in which the biryani will be prepared on dum and served. Put the chicken into the handi and make a neat layer of it. Scatter half the remaining fried onions and some coriander leaves.

16 Next add the cooked rice and smoothen it out neatly.

17 Heat the milk in a pan and once it's hot, stir in the saffron strands. Set aside for a while to infuse the milk.

18 Pour the saffron-infused milk over the rice, sprinkle the remaining browned onions and some more coriander leaves and add a dollop of butter.

19 Insert the handle of a long ladle into the biryani all the way to the bottom of the pan and draw a cross pattern through the layers of the biryani to get them to intermingle with each other.

TO COOK ON DUM

20 Now for the dum, make the sealing dough by adding just enough water to the wholewheat flour and kneading it to make a firm, pliable dough.

21 Roll the sealing dough into a long, slender roll with the palms of your hands. Place the rolls over the rim of the handi, pressing down gently to help it stay in place.

22 Once the entire rim or mouth of the handi is covered with the ring of dough, cover the handi with its lid and press it down firmly into the dough to create a seal. Carefully overlap the overhanging dough on to the lid to seal it completely.

23 Put the sealed handi on high heat for about 5 minutes to allow the steam to build up inside. Turn the heat down to the barest of simmers. Put the biryani on dum for about 30 minutes, by which time the chicken will be falling off the bone, the rice perfectly cooked and delicately flavoured with the complex marinade and whole spices.

24 Leave the handi to rest for about 10 minutes and then break open the seal.

25 Serve the biryani with any raita of choice and an onion and green chilli salad.

Bhuna Kukda

(Slow-Fried Chicken in Whole Spices and Curd)

6–7 SERVINGS

A robust dish of chicken cooked in mustard oil and whole spices, this is a great example of the rustic use of whole spices in Indian cuisines. A super way to cook all varieties of meat.

Method

1 Cut the chicken into medium to large pieces on the bone. Clean and wash thoroughly, and dry on kitchen towels.

THE CURRY

2 To make the base for the dish, put the mustard oil in a kadhai or deep sauté pan on high heat till it smokes, to burn off its bitterness. Once the oil is smoking and almost clear in colour, take the pan off the heat and cool the oil.

3 Return the pan to medium heat, add the whole spices and bay leaf and sauté, till they crackle and release their aromas. Now add the whole garlic cloves and sauté them, till they turn golden brown.

4 Drain the soaked red chillies and stir them into the pan. Sauté for a few minutes more or till they are a deep, rich, red colour and robust in their aroma. Add the turmeric powder and coriander powder to the pan and sauté them, till well toasted.

5 Sprinkle in a little water and deglaze the pan. Bhuno the masala a few times adding a little water each time the spices are drying out, till the masala is a rich, yellow-brown and the oil has risen to the surface.

6 Turn up the heat and add 3 chicken pieces at a time. Fry them in the hot mustard oil-based masala, till they are richly golden in colour.

7 Add the salt and sugar to aid the caramelization of the chicken and to balance the heat of the chillies. Stir in the vinegar and sauté till the chicken is deep golden brown.

8 Turn the heat down, cover the pan and let the chicken cook for 30 minutes or till it is 80 per cent cooked through.

9 Uncover the pan and stir everything together a few times, scraping up the rich pan deposits stuck to the base.

10 Add the whisked curd, turn up the heat and fry the chicken in the curd and spices to the point when most of the curd is absorbed, the masala gravy is thick, coats the chicken perfectly and the golden mustard oil rises to the surface.

11 Turn the heat down, cover the pan and simmer the chicken, till it is almost coming off the bone and is perfectly cooked. Uncover the pan and turn up the heat to reduce the thick masala.

Ingredients

1 kg chicken	10 dried red Guntur chillies, soaked in water for 30 minutes
THE CURRY BASE	½ tsp turmeric powder
4 tbsp mustard oil	1 tsp coriander powder
½" cassia stick	¾–1 tsp salt
1 tsp cumin seeds	½ tsp sugar
6 cloves	2 tsp malt vinegar
2 brown cardamoms	1 cup whisked curd
4 green cardamoms	Juice of ½ a lime
1 bay leaf	3 tsp chopped fresh coriander leaves
12 garlic cloves, kept whole	

12 Mix well to ensure that the masala coats the chicken richly. Squeeze in the lime juice and sprinkle the coriander leaves.

13 Check for a balance of flavours: the chicken should be tender and succulent, full of the robust, yet delicate flavour of the mustard, whole spice and curd-based masala. The thick masala needs to be spicy hot; the curd and lime should help in balancing the mustard oil and spices perfectly. The mustard oil in turn, should create an oily sheen on the surface.

14 Serve the bhuna kukda hot with tandoori roti.

Butter Chicken

3–4 SERVINGS

Butter chicken is actually of Mughlai origin, but over the years it has been keenly adopted by several different cultures and cuisines. Traditionally, it is made with charcoal-grilled chicken tikka or tandoori chicken pieces simmered in a rich buttery tomato gravy. However, this version is typically made in homes and uses fried marinated chicken instead. In its modern avatar, a grill can be used as well, for a brilliant, smoky, buttery flavour to this classic creation.

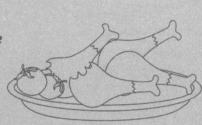

Method

1 Wash the chicken and trim it. Cut it into tikka-sized chunks.

THE MARINADE

2 Combine all the marinade ingredients in a small bowl. Put the chicken into a large glass or plastic bowl. Add the marinade and mix it well into the chicken with your hands. Cover and leave to marinate in the refrigerator for a couple of hours.

3 While the chicken is marinating, prepare the rich tomato gravy.

THE RICH TOMATO GRAVY

4 Blanch the tomatoes, peel them and purée the flesh.

5 Heat a medium-sized sauté pan and add the oil and butter. Keep the pan on medium heat, till the butter is foaming. The oil prevents the butter from burning as it has a much higher smoking point.

6 Once the foam subsides somewhat, add the chopped ginger and green chillies and sauté for a couple of minutes on medium heat.

7 Add the spice powders and sauté, till they are aromatic and richly coloured.

8 Now add the fresh tomato purée and stir to mix with the spices. Simmer on low heat, till the tomato gravy is thick and has a rich, deep red colour and the oil rises to the surface.

9 Season well with salt and add the sugar. Stir through and simmer for a few minutes longer. Turn off the heat and set the gravy aside to mature.

TO COOK THE CHICKEN

10 Remove the marinated chicken from the refrigerator and bring to room temperature. Season with salt and mix well.

11 Heat a heavy non-stick frying pan and add a few drops of refined oil and the butter.

12 Once the butter is hot, add a few chicken pieces at a time and sear them on high heat, till they develop a rich caramelized crust and are slightly charred around the edges. Remove to a plate and repeat with the remaining pieces.

13 Now, return all the seared chicken pieces to the pan and fry them all together. Add the sugar, lime juice and any remaining marinade. Continue to fry the chicken, till it is almost fully cooked and turns a lovely, charred, golden brown.

Ingredients

500 gms boneless chicken	1 tsp cumin powder	1 tsp hot red chilli powder
1 tsp salt	½ tsp turmeric powder	½ tsp cumin powder
A few drops of refined oil	1 tsp hot red chilli powder	1 tsp coriander powder
50 gms butter	Juice of 1 lime	¾ tsp salt
½ tsp sugar	**THE RICH TOMATO GRAVY**	½ tsp sugar, to balance the acidity of the tomatoes
Juice of ½ a lime	7–8 ripe red tomatoes	
THE MARINADE	A few drops of refined oil	4–5 tbsp full cream
3 tsp ginger-garlic paste	50 gms butter	**THE GARNISH**
½ an onion, puréed	½" ginger, chopped fine	2–3 tsp chopped fresh coriander leaves
4 tbsp whisked curd	2 green chillies, chopped fine	
1 tsp coriander powder	½ tsp turmeric powder	A knob of butter

14 Add the thick, spicy tomato gravy to the chicken and deglaze the pan to lift up those intense pan deposits. Cook on medium heat, stirring well to make sure the chicken is fully submerged and coated in the delicious gravy.

15 Simmer uncovered to reduce the gravy.

16 Turn the heat down to a simmer and add the thick cream. Stir through to combine and cook for about 5 minutes to blend well.

17 Check for a balance of flavours: the gravy should be rich and buttery, bursting with the spices and concentrated tomatoes; the chicken, perfectly tender and packed with the rich flavours of the creamy tomato gravy.

18 Sprinkle some coriander leaves, add a knob of butter and enjoy this home-style butter chicken with naan or tandoori roti.

Coorgi Gawti Koli
(Coorgi Country Chicken Curry)
6 SERVINGS

An exotic dish from Coorg, which boasts of bold and robust flavours, the country chicken in this recipe complements the spices perfectly, or vice-versa.

Method

1 Cut the chicken into medium-sized curry pieces, wash and trim the pieces. Drain thoroughly.

THE MARINADE

2 Combine the marinade ingredients in a small bowl and mix, till well blended. Put the chicken into a bowl and rub the marinade in thoroughly to coat the pieces evenly with the spices. Cover and put into the refrigerator to marinate for about an hour.

THE COORGI MASALA PASTE

3 To make the Coorgi masala paste, heat a medium-sized frying pan for a couple of minutes and add all the masala paste ingredients to it. Dry-roast them on medium heat, till they release their natural oils, are aromatic and have begun to turn a rich, deep brown.

4 Once the spices, coconut and aromatics are smoky, slightly charred and robust in their aroma, turn off the heat and transfer them to a mortar or spice grinder. Add a little water and grind to make a fine, dark brownish-black, coconut-based paste. Set aside.

THE CURRY

5 Now, to make the curry base, heat a large, deep pan and add the oil. When the oil is hot, add the mustard and fenugreek seeds and sauté them on medium heat, till they crackle and turn nutty.

6 Add the red chillies, curry leaves and onions to the pan and fry them in the hot oil, till the chillies and curry leaves are crisp, and the onion is lightly caramelized and golden.

7 Turn up the heat slightly and add the Coorgi masala paste. Fry the paste for a couple of minutes, till most of its moisture has evaporated and the masala begins to stick to the base of the pan.

8 Add a little water to deglaze the pan, scraping up the rich, caramelized pan deposits that are stuck to the base and bhuno the masala repeatedly with water, till it is smooth and homogenous in consistency, and the oil rises to the surface.

9 Once the oil has surfaced and the masala is dark brownish-black, add the chopped tomatoes, salt and sugar and fry, till the tomatoes are completely broken down and well amalgamated with the masala.

10 Stir in the tamarind extract and sauté for couple of minutes, till well blended.

11 Remove the chicken from the refrigerator, season it well with salt and then add it to the masala base. Turn up the heat and fry the chicken in the masala, till it is well coated and richly browned all over.

12 Now add enough water to cover the chicken and stir everything together. Bring the dark brown

The Chakh le India Cookbook

Ingredients

1 medium to large country chicken	1½ tsp coriander seeds	A few curry leaves
½ tsp salt	1½ tsp whole black peppercorns	2 medium-sized onions, chopped
THE MARINADE	4–5 cloves	2 tomatoes, seeded and chopped fine
1 tsp turmeric powder	½" cassia stick	½ tsp salt
1 tsp red chilli powder	½ tsp turmeric powder	¾–1 tsp sugar
3 tsp ginger-garlic paste	1 tsp red chilli powder	4 tbsp thick tamarind extract (see page 10)
2 tsp refined oil	1 tsp salt	**THE TEMPERING**
THE COORGI MASALA PASTE	**THE CURRY BASE**	½ tsp mustard seeds
1 fresh coconut, grated	3 tsp refined oil	3–4 dried red chillies
6 garlic cloves	1 tsp mustard seeds	A few curry leaves
½" ginger	½ tsp fenugreek seeds	
1 tsp cumin seeds	4–5 hot dried red chillies	

curry to a boil, turn the heat down, cover and simmer the chicken for 2–2½ hours, till it is perfectly tender and cooked through; the gravy should be semi-thick and the oil should rise to the surface.

13 When the chicken is tender, uncover the pan and reduce the gravy to concentrate it. Stir the semi-thick curry a few times to mix well.

14 Now, heat the oil for the tempering in a small frying pan and add the tempering ingredients. Fry them on medium heat, till crisp, crackled and aromatic.

15 Pour the tempering into the simmering curry. Stir it in and turn off the heat.

16 Check for a balance of flavours: the chicken should be perfectly tender and full of the tang of the hot, spicy gravy. The semi-thick gravy should be really peppery, with the spices and aromatics giving it a robust and intensely flavoursome character. The rich, nutty sweetness of the coconut should come through well, in order to balance the heat of the pepper perfectly. The crisp, fried tempering ingredients should lend a lovely contrast of texture and colour to the dish.

17 Serve with steamed rice.

Chicken Recipes

Kerala Chicken Stew

* *

Yet another classic dish from Kerala, this coconut milk-based dish is exotically simple in its character. It's both delicate and aromatic and brings together all the ingredients in a lush, nutty-sweet manner. In Kerala, it's eaten with steamed appams but it can also be teamed up with rice. A real cracker of a stew!

Ingredients

THE CHICKEN

1 kg chicken without skin

2 medium-sized potatoes, peeled and cubed

3–4 tsp malt vinegar

½ tsp salt

THE GARAM MASALA

3 green cardamoms

½" cassia stick

4 cloves

THE STEW BASE

2 tsp refined oil

1 onion, chopped

6 garlic cloves, chopped

½" ginger, chopped

3 hot green chillies, slit

¾ tsp salt

2 cups thick coconut milk (see page 10)

THE TEMPERING

2 tsp refined oil

A few curry leaves

½ tsp mustard seeds

2 hot green chillies

Method

THE CHICKEN

1 Cut the chicken into medium-sized pieces and wash.

2 Next, par-cook the chicken and potatoes. Put them in a pressure cooker with the vinegar, salt and 2½ cups of water. Cook for 10–12 minutes on low heat, after the cooker reaches full pressure. Turn off the heat and leave to cool in the closed cooker. This technique is used to par-cook the meat and vegetables and create a delicious stock that forms the medium of the stew.

THE GARAM MASALA

3 Grind the whole spices in a mortar or grinder, to make a semi-coarse powder.

THE STEW

4 To make the base, heat a deep sauté pan and add the oil. Once the oil is hot, add the onions, garlic, ginger and green chillies and sauté on medium heat, till they are a light golden.

5 Add the freshly ground garam masala to the sautéed base. Fry gently for a few minutes on medium heat, till the pan exudes a wonderful aroma.

6 Now open the pressure cooker and add the chicken, potatoes and stock to the pan with the aromatic spice base.

7 Sprinkle in the salt, and simmer gently, till the chicken is almost cooked.

8 Pour in the coconut milk, stirring gently to combine. The stew will turn milky and have a delicately sweet aroma with this addition.

9 Simmer covered, on the lowest possible heat, till the chicken is almost coming off the bone and the potatoes are perfectly soft.

10 Turn off the heat and leave to cool while preparing the temper. Heat the oil in a small tempering pan or spoon. Add the remaining tempering ingredients and fry on high heat, till they crackle.

11 Pour the hot oil and tempering into the stew and stir through to combine nicely.

12 Check for salt and a balance of flavours: the stew should look delicate and exotic with the lush coconut milk and be aromatic with the spices.

13 Serve with lemon rice.

Andhra Chicken Lollipops Pg 42

Bhuna Kukda Pg 46

Handi Biryani
Pg 55

Khatta Meetha
Kadhai Murgh Pg 60

Handi Biryani
(Chicken and Vegetable Biryani)
7–8 SERVINGS

If there ever was a rustic, peasant-style biryani, this is it! A complete meal in itself with layers of meat, rice and vegetables, it's just the perfect dish to feed large numbers of people, say after a game or at a picnic. Any combination of meat, vegetables and spices can be used according to preference.

Ingredients

THE RICE

500 gms basmati rice

3 tsp refined oil

3 green cardamoms

1 brown cardamom

4–5 cloves

1 tsp cumin seeds

6–8 whole black peppercorns

½" cassia stick

1 bay leaf

½ tsp salt

THE VEGETABLE LAYER

3 tsp refined oil

1 tsp cumin seeds

1 large onion, julienned

3 potatoes, boiled, peeled and cut into 1" cubes

2 green capsicums, sliced fine

A knob of butter

½ tsp salt

THE CHICKEN LAYER

1 kg chicken without skin

2 tsp refined oil

1 tsp cumin seeds

3 hot dried red chillies

1 medium-sized onion, chopped

2 tbsp ginger-garlic paste

1 tsp turmeric powder

1 tsp red chilli powder

1½ tsp coriander powder

¾ tsp salt

3 tomatoes, seeded and chopped into thin petals

A pinch of sugar

½ cup whisked curd

Juice of 1 lime

TO LAYER THE BIRYANI

1 cup milk

A few saffron strands

2 tbsp butter

3–4 tsp chopped fresh coriander leaves

Juice of ½ a lime

THE RICE

1 To make this rustic chicken and vegetable biryani, start off by par-cooking the basmati rice. Wash the rice in several changes of water, till most of the excess starch is removed. Soak it in fresh water for 10 minutes.

2 Heat the oil in a large pan. Add the whole spices and bay leaf and sauté them on medium heat, till crackling, coloured and aromatic.

3 Drain the rice and add it to the pan. Fry the rice in the hot oil and whole spices, to toast it and bring out its aroma.

4 Once the rice is toasted and aromatic, with a nice oily sheen on its surface, add 2 litres of boiling water with the salt and stir it well, picking up any grains stuck to the base of the pan. Bring to a boil and cook the rice, uncovered, till it is about 80 per cent cooked and the grains are perfectly separated.

5 Strain it well and spread it out gently on a large tray or platter to cool.

THE VEGETABLE LAYER

6 For the vegetable layer, heat the oil in a medium-sized frying pan and add the cumin seeds. Sauté them on medium heat, till crackling and fragrant. Then add the onion and sauté it on high heat, till it's lightly charred, smoky and soft.

7 Next add the boiled, cubed potatoes and fry them for a few minutes to colour them lightly.

8 Add the sliced capsicums and fry on high heat to char them, giving them a lovely smoky flavour and to soften them slightly.

9 Season the vegetables with salt and then add a knob of butter. Stir a few times, then turn off the heat and set aside.

THE CHICKEN LAYER

10 To prepare the chicken layer, first cut it into medium-sized curry pieces and wash well. Drain thoroughly.

11 Heat a large frying pan, add the oil and swirl the pan to coat it well. Once the oil is hot, add the cumin seeds and crackle them on medium heat to release their aroma. Add the red chillies and fry them, till crisp and aromatic.

12 Add the onion to the pan and sauté it on medium heat, till it takes on a lovely, light, golden brown colour. Stir in the ginger-garlic paste and sauté it with the onions, till it turns light golden.

13 Mix in the spice powders, turn up the heat and toast them, till they are intensely aromatic and dry.

14 Once the spices and aromatics are completely dry, add a little water to deglaze the pan and lift up all the rich, concentrated pan deposits. Bhuno the masala repeatedly on medium heat, using water, till the base is a rich, golden yellow-red and the oil has risen to the surface.

15 When the base is properly cooked, turn up the heat and add the chicken. Season the pieces well with salt and fry them in the rich aromatic spice base, till they are richly browned and have taken on the colour and flavour of the masala.

16 Now turn the heat down slightly and continue to fry the chicken in the base, till richly coated with the masala. Sprinkle in a few drops of water to deglaze the rich, meaty pan deposits once more.

17 Stir in the tomatoes and fry them with the chicken, till they begin to soften and disintegrate slightly. Add the sugar to balance the acidity of the tomatoes and further caramelize the chicken.

18 Stir the ingredients together to combine well and create a rich caramel of the meat juices, tomatoes and masala in the base of the pan.

19 Finally, add the curd and deglaze the pan, scraping and incorporating all the concentrated juices into a thick, curd-and-tomato-based masala gravy.

20 Turn the heat down, stir everything together, add a little water, cover the pan and simmer the chicken, till it's perfectly cooked and tender.

21 Once the chicken is done, uncover the pan, turn up the heat and reduce the thick gravy to concentrate it.

22 The gravy should be semi-coating in consistency, with the curd, tomatoes and spices coming through nicely and the chicken wonderfully tender and aromatic.

23 Squeeze some lime juice to lift the flavours, turn off the heat and set aside.

TO LAYER THE BIRYANI

24 Now that all the different components of this unusual biryani are cooked, the next step is to layer them and complete the process by using the dum technique.

25 Take a handi or a pan with a wide base and narrow mouth that's large enough to take all the components. Put a spoonful of the thick chicken gravy at the bottom, then add an inch-deep layer of the rice.

26 Put all the chicken over the rice layer and smoothen it out to level it in one thick layer. Next, add a little more rice to cover the chicken and then spread the vegetables on top of the rice layer. Smoothen out the vegetables as well.

27 Finally, add the remaining rice over the top to finish as the last layer.

28 Bring the milk to a boil in a pan. Turn off the heat and add the saffron strands. Wait for around 10 minutes for the milk to be infused with the saffron. Once the milk is almost cool, add the butter and swirl the milk to melt it.

29 Pour the saffron infused milk over the top layer of rice, sprinkle coriander leaves and squeeze the lime juice on top.

COOKING ON DUM

30 To put the biryani on dum, place the pan on medium heat and cover it with a tight-fitting lid, making sure there is no way for the steam to escape. Finally, place a heavy mortar or any other heavy object on the pan to create a seal.

31 Raise the temperature of the pan on medium heat, till it is hot to the touch, then turn the temperature to a bare simmer, and let the biryani cook on dum for about 30 minutes.

32 Once the biryani is cooked to perfection, remove the heavy object and carefully uncover the handi.

33 Serve this amazingly rustic, home-style, multi-layered biryani steaming hot with a chilled raita.

Himachali Tava Murgh
(Himachali Pan-Fried Chicken)

4–5 SERVINGS

A deliciously tender tava-style recipe that is really simple to put together. The chicken can be grilled instead of fried, to get a smoky tandoori version as well. A perfect party dish, it can be marinated and kept in the refrigerator and cooked instantly. An oven-roasted version is equally delectable.

Method

1 Cut the chicken into large pieces. Wash thoroughly, drain and dry on kitchen towels.

THE MARINADE

2 Put the hung curd, cream and ginger-garlic paste in a large glass bowl.

3 Dry-roast the whole spices and bay leaf and grind them in a mortar or grinder, till the masala is aromatic.

4 Add the ground garam masala to the bowl and mix, till well blended.

5 Add the chicken with the lime juice and massage the mixture into the chicken thoroughly to ensure that the marinade coats the chicken well. Cover and leave to marinate in the refrigerator for 2–4 hours.

6 Once done, remove the chicken from the refrigerator and bring it to room temperature.

TO COOK THE CHICKEN

7 Heat the oil in a hot frying pan. Add the chicken pieces, a couple at a time, and sear well on high heat. When the chicken takes on a lovely, light golden brown colour and the natural sugars of the meat begin to caramelize, turn the pieces over to brown the other side. Remove the seared chicken pieces from the pan and put them on a plate. Repeat with the remaining pieces of chicken.

8 Return all the seared chicken to the pan. Toss a few times and season well with salt. The marinade will now start to cook, forming a thick, clotted masala in the pan.

9 Add a few drops of water to deglaze the rich pan juices clinging to the bottom.

10 Cover the pan and turn the heat down to medium-low. Let the chicken cook in its own juices with the thick masala gravy becoming richer and more concentrated as the bird cooks in the steam.

11 Cook the chicken, till the flesh is almost coming off the bone. Uncover the pan to reduce the gravy slightly and concentrate it.

12 Check for a balance of flavours: the chicken should be tender and the thick masala should cling to it. It should also be slightly tangy from the curd and delicately aromatic from the garam masala and the pungent ginger and garlic paste. The oil should have risen to the surface, signalling that the spices are fully cooked.

Ingredients

1 chicken	4–5 cloves	**THE GARNISH**
THE MARINADE	1 bay leaf	2–3 tsp chopped fresh coriander leaves
2 cups hung curd	Juice of 1 lime	4–5 lime wedges
2 tbsp fresh cream	**TO COOK**	
2 tbsp ginger-garlic paste	1 tbsp refined oil	
6 green cardamoms	¾ tsp salt	
2 brown cardamoms	Juice of ½ a lime	
1" cassia stick	**THE TEMPERING**	
½ tsp whole black peppercorns	2 tsp ghee	
½ tsp cumin seeds	3 dried red chillies	
1 tsp coriander seeds	A small handful of fresh coriander leaves	

13 For a quick tempering, heat the ghee in a cooking ladle, till hot. Add the remaining tempering ingredients and fry on medium heat, till the chillies and coriander leaves are crisp. Spoon the tempering over the tava murgh and then squeeze in some more lime juice, to lift all the flavours.

14 Garnish with chopped coriander leaves and lime wedges and serve straight away with hot parantha.

Khatta Meetha Kadhai Murgh

(Sweet and Sour Chicken with Stir-Fried Vegetables)

6 SERVINGS

A perfect dish for a Sunday brunch or picnic, it works very well for large numbers of people. One of the tricks in this recipe is to keep the vegetables crisp and full of flavour by stir-frying them separately. As a variation, a much simpler marinade with less complex spices can also be used.

Method

1 Cut the chicken into 8 large pieces and trim any excess fat. Wash well, drain and dry on kitchen towels.

THE MARINADE

2 To make the marinade for the chicken, heat a small frying pan. Add the oil and when hot, add all the marinade ingredients except the tamarind extract and jaggery. Fry the spices and aromatics in the hot oil on medium heat, till they release their aroma.

3 Once the spices and aromatics are fragrant, turn off the heat and transfer them to a heavy mortar or grinder. Add the tamarind extract and jaggery and grind to make a deep, reddish brown paste that's really fine and smooth in consistency.

4 Taste a little of the marinade to check for a balance between sour, sweet and spicy. If it is too hot, add a little more tamarind extract and mix it in well. The paste should have a distinct tang to it.

5 Put the chicken into a bowl, add the tangy marinade and rub it into the pieces well, making sure that the marinade penetrates the chicken and coats it evenly. Cover and put into the refrigerator to marinate for 2–4 hours.

TO COOK THE CHICKEN

6 To cook the chicken, remove the marinated chicken from the refrigerator and bring it to room temperature. Season it with salt.

7 Heat a large non-stick frying pan. Add the refined oil and a knob of butter and heat well, till the butter melts and the foam subsides.

8 Add half the chicken pieces to the pan and sear them on one side, till a rich, brown caramelized crust is formed. Turn the pieces over and sear them on the second side and then toss the pieces on all sides so that they turn a rich brown colour on all sides. Remove the browned pieces to a plate and repeat with the remaining pieces.

9 Once all the chicken has been browned and the marinade has formed a rich, thick, dark brown coating, return all the pieces to the pan.

10 Cover the pan and turn the heat down. Simmer the chicken on low heat for about 30 minutes, to allow it to cook to a succulent perfection in its own juices.

Ingredients

1 chicken without skin	½" cassia stick	2 medium-sized onions, cut into fairly broad juliennes
½ tsp salt	3 cloves	1 large red pepper, seeded and sliced semi-thin
3 tsp refined oil	½ tsp whole black peppercorns	3 green chillies, chopped
A knob of butter	½ tsp turmeric powder	¼ tsp salt

THE TANGY, SWEET, SPICY MARINADE

1 tsp refined oil
6 garlic cloves
½" ginger
6-8 hot dried red chillies
½ tsp cumin seeds
1 tsp coriander seeds

1 tsp red chilli powder
½ tsp salt
4 tbsp thick tamarind extract (see page 10)
½ tsp grated jaggery

THE KADHAI VEGETABLES

3 tsp refined oil

THE GARNISH

Juice of ½ a lime
2 tsp chopped fresh coriander leaves
1 spring onion (green part only), chopped semi-fine

THE KADHAI VEGETABLES

11 To stir-fry the vegetables, heat a wok or frying pan and add the oil. Swirl the pan to coat it well.

12 Toss the onions into the wok, charring them nicely for a delicious smoky flavour.

13 Once they are nicely charred but firm in texture, add the red pepper and green chillies and toss them on high heat to both char and soften them slightly, while keeping them juicy and crisp. Season with salt and remove to a plate. Set aside.

TO COMPLETE THE DISH

14 Once the chicken is cooked and tender, uncover the pan and turn up the heat to reduce the thick coating masala even further and concentrate it.

15 When the masala is really thick, coating the chicken well and the oil has risen to the surface, add the stir-fried vegetables to the pan and mix everything together.

16 Now, squeeze some lime juice to lift the flavours and sprinkle the coriander leaves and spring onion greens for a little colour and herby freshness and serve the spicy and tangy kadhai murgh with hot naan.

Murgh Badami
(Almond Chicken)
6 SERVINGS

The nawabs and other royals of India were renowned for their refined culinary tastes. Legend has it that they encouraged royal cooks to experiment with ingredients, and are acknowledged for taking Indian cuisines to fantastic heights. This recipe is fabulously refined, creamy and luxurious, with a delicate flavour and colour. Lovers of Mughlai food are sure to fall for this unusual dish.

Method

1 Cut the chicken into medium-sized, curry pieces. Wash well and drain. Set aside.

THE GARAM MASALA

2 To prepare the coarse garam masala, dry-roast all the whole spices in a small frying pan, till they release their natural oils and smell aromatic.

3 Transfer them to a heavy mortar or grinder and grind them to a fairly coarse powder, along with the nutmeg. Reserve.

THE CURRY

4 Now, to create the base for the dish, heat the ghee in a deep pan. Once it is nutty in its aroma, add the onion. Sauté on medium heat, till it is soft and begins to take on a slight colour.

5 Add the ginger and garlic to the pan and sauté, till they are soft and aromatic.

6 Sprinkle in the coarse garam masala and sauté on medium heat, till it becomes intensely fragrant.

7 Stir in the spice powders, turn up the heat and sauté, till they are well toasted and the base is fairly dry.

8 Add a little water and deglaze the pan, lifting up the rich pan juices stuck to the base. Bhuno the

aromatic spice base a few times with water, till it is well combined and the oil rises to the surface.

9 Mix in the whisked curd, turn the heat down and simmer for a few minutes to cook it with the spices.

10 When the oil surfaces again, add the almond paste to the pan and mix it in.

11 Simmer the thick, yellowy gravy for a few minutes longer to blend well.

12 Put the milk into a small pan and bring it to a boil. Then turn off the heat and add the saffron strands to the milk.

13 Stir the milk a few times and add it to the thick simmering gravy. Mix the saffron-infused milk into the gravy, giving it a beautifully light yellow, creamy colour.

14 Add the chicken to the lush, simmering gravy, throw in the dried apricots, season with salt and stir everything well to combine.

15 When all the chicken pieces are fully submerged in the curry, bring the pan up to a gentle boil. Turn the heat down to low and poach the chicken in the simmering curry, till it's perfectly cooked.

The Chakh le India Cookbook

Ingredients

1 chicken, without skin	½" ginger, chopped fine
THE GARAM MASALA	6 garlic cloves, chopped fine
½ tsp whole black peppercorns	1 tsp coriander powder
2 brown cardamoms	½ tsp turmeric powder
6 green cardamoms	1 tsp cumin powder
½" cassia stick	1 cup whisked curd
6 cloves	3–4 tbsp almond paste (see note)
A pinch of freshly grated nutmeg	½ cup milk
THE CURRY BASE	A few saffron strands
1 tbsp ghee	10 dried apricots
1 large onion, chopped fine	1 tsp salt

16 Once the chicken is cooked to perfection and the oil surfaces nicely, stir the semi-thick gravy a few times to mix well, and turn off the heat.

17 Remove the cooked chicken with a spoon or tongs and put them into a serving bowl; the chicken should be really soft and tender from the gently poaching in the curd and milk. Keep warm.

18 Strain the semi-thick gravy through a sieve and into a heavy saucepan, pressing on the solids in the sieve to extract their entire flavour and make a perfectly smooth and very refined gravy.

19 Simmer the gravy on low heat for a few minutes to reduce it slightly and concentrate it. Once it is hot and perfectly balanced, turn off the heat and pour the hot refined gravy over the warm chicken pieces.

20 Check for a balance of flavours: the chicken should be beautifully tender, moist from within and delicately flavoured with the spices and aromatics of the curry as well as the nutty sweetness of the almonds. The curd and milk should have lent creaminess to the gravy, helping to tenderize the chicken too. The rich nutty creamy gravy should be a lovely golden yellow and infused with the complex yet delicate combination of spices and aromatics. On the whole, the curry should be creamy, delicate and really refined.

21 Serve it with hot tandoori roti or laccha parantha.

NOTE: To make the almond paste, blanch almonds, peel them and grind them to make a fine paste with a little water.

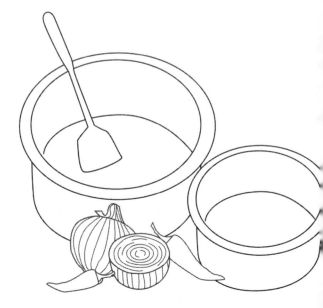

Murgh Noorjehani

(Mughlai Chicken in a Saffron and Milk Gravy)

6 SERVINGS

....

A Mughlai recipe with melt-in-your-mouth chicken, this dish is special for its refined gravy with the delicate saffron and dried fruits. A perfect dish for formal parties, owing to its delicate and rich flavours.

Method

1 Cut the chicken into medium-sized curry pieces. Trim, wash well and drain thoroughly.

THE MARINADE

2 Dry-roast all the marinade ingredients except the curd in a hot frying pan on medium heat, till they release their natural oils and are aromatic.

3 Transfer them to a heavy mortar or grinder, add a little water and grind them to make a fine paste.

4 Put the chicken into a bowl, add the masala paste and whisked curd and massage it into the chicken really well. Cover and put into the refrigerator to marinate for 3–4 hours.

THE CURRY

5 Once the chicken is marinated, remove it from the refrigerator and bring to room temperature. Season with salt.

6 Heat a deep pan and add 1 tsp of ghee and the bay leaf and let it crackle. Stir in the onion purée and sauté on medium heat, till it turns light golden.

7 Add the marinated chicken to the pan and fry it in the hot fragrant ghee, till the chicken begins to take on a very light golden colour. Take care not to caramelize it in excess, as this dish should be yellow-white when ready.

8 While the chicken is frying in the ghee and marinade, heat the milk in a small pan till tepid and add the saffron strands to infuse the milk.

9 When the chicken is coloured well and coated in the thick marinade-based masala, cover the pan and cook on low heat for about 20–25 minutes or till the chicken is almost cooked and the ghee has risen to the surface.

10 Pour in the saffron-infused milk and stir gently to combine all the ingredients well.

11 Simmer uncovered for another 20 minutes or till the chicken is cooked to perfect tenderness and the rich curd and milk-based gravy is reduced, has a lovely, saffron yellow colour and coats the chicken.

12 Heat the remaining 1 tsp of ghee in a small frying pan. Fry the raisins and almonds on medium heat, till the raisins are golden and plump and the almonds wonderfully glossy and nutty in their aroma. Add them to the chicken and mix well to combine.

Ingredients

1 chicken	**THE CURRY BASE**
1 tsp salt	1 tsp ghee
THE MARINADE	1 bay leaf
6–8 garlic cloves	2 medium-sized onions, puréed
½" ginger	½ cup milk
1 tsp fennel seeds	A few saffron strands
1" cassia stick	¼–½ tsp salt
4 cloves	A small handful of seedless raisins
2 brown cardamoms, seeds only	10–12 almonds, blanched, peeled and ground to a paste with a little water
3 green cardamoms, seeds only	
2 cups whisked curd	

13 Remove the bay leaf, turn off the heat and stir everything one last time. Taste and add salt if required.

14 Check for a balance of flavours: the gravy should be thick and concentrated, wonderfully aromatic with the fennel, saffron, curd, milk and spices. The chicken should be really tender and full of the amazing flavours of the rich, milky saffron and aromatic spice gravy.

15 Serve hot with tandoori roti or parantha.

Pahadi Murgh
(Uttarakhand/Himachal Herb-Flavoured Chicken)

6 SERVINGS

··

A fantastic fresh hara or herby green masala takes this Himachal recipe to another level. A classic example of the rustic pahadi or mountain recipe with succulent chicken in a thick and intensely flavoured green gravy, this one is a must!

Method

1 Cut the chicken into curry-sized pieces and trim. Wash the chicken and drain thoroughly.

THE MARINADE

2 Combine the marinade ingredients in a small bowl and mix well.

3 Put the chicken pieces into a bowl and rub in the marinade really well. Cover and put into the refrigerator to marinate for 2–4 hours.

THE PAHADI GREEN MASALA

4 To make the fresh green masala, heat the oil in a frying pan and add all the masala ingredients, starting with the aromatics and ending with the spice powders. Fry the ingredients in the hot oil, till they exude their aroma and change colour.

5 Turn off the heat and transfer to a mortar or spice grinder. Add a little water and grind to make a fine, vivid green paste. The masala paste should be hot and spicy and smell wonderfully fresh with all the herbs and spring onions. Set aside.

THE CURRY

6 Once the chicken is marinated, remove it from the refrigerator and bring to room temperature.

7 To create the curry base, heat the ghee in a deep pan. When it's bubbling hot, add the whole spices and fry for a minute, till coloured and aromatic.

8 Stir in the chopped onion and sauté on medium heat, till soft and lightly coloured.

9 Turn up the heat a little and add the green masala paste to the pan. Fry the paste with the onion and whole spices, till it begins to turn dark green.

10 Add a little water and bhuno the masala on high heat, till it's a rich, deep green and the ghee rises to the surface.

11 Once the masala is well cooked and amalgamated, add the marinated chicken to the pan. Season well with salt, turn up the heat and fry the chicken in the masala for 10–12 minutes or till it is deliciously coated in the masala base and is a lovely, greenish golden colour.

12 Turn the heat down to medium and stir the chicken a few times to mix everything together. Add the whisked curd and fry with the chicken for a few minutes, till the gravy is thick and almost fully absorbed.

Ingredients

1 kg chicken	1 tsp cumin seeds	**THE CURRY BASE**
1 tsp salt	½ tsp whole black peppercorns	1 tbsp ghee
MARINADE	½" cassia stick	2 brown cardamoms
1 tsp turmeric powder	4–5 cloves	½" cassia stick
1 tsp medium-hot red chilli powder	½ tsp fennel seeds	1 onion, chopped fine
1–2 tsp refined oil	4 hot green chillies	¼ tsp salt
THE PAHADI GREEN MASALA	½ cup chopped fresh coriander leaves	1 cup whisked curd
2 tsp refined oil	2 spring onions, with some of the tender greens, chopped	½ cup milk
½" ginger	1 tsp red chilli powder	1 spring onion (white part only) sliced into rings
6 garlic cloves	½ tsp turmeric powder	A knob of butter
1½ tsp coriander seeds		

13 Next, add the milk and stir everything a couple of times to mix. Bring to a boil and turn the heat down to a simmer. Cover the pan and gently simmer the chicken, till it's deliciously tender, almost coming off the bone and the oil has risen to the surface. By now, the gravy will be a rich, deep green in colour.

14 When the chicken is thoroughly cooked and meltingly tender, uncover the pan, turn up the heat a little and reduce the gravy to concentrate and thicken it slightly.

15 Mix in the spring onion rings and a knob of butter and stir through a couple of times.

16 Turn off the heat and check for a balance of flavours: the chicken should be meltingly tender and full of the delicious spicy and creamy green herb masala. The warm spices, such as the pepper and cloves should come through the buttery curd and milk-based gravy, intensely flavoursome and complex.

17 Serve hot with tandoori rotis.

Tandoori Chicken

4 SERVINGS

Tandoori chicken is possibly one of the world's most famous dishes!! It's hard to beat the butch, spicy and charred flavours of the succulent chicken cooked over charcoal! The tandoori paste can be preserved in the refrigerator for a few weeks and is amazingly versatile.

Method

1 Cut the chicken into 8 main sections—2 drumsticks, 2 thighs, 4 breast pieces and the body or carcass cut into 2 pieces. Wash and trim the pieces and dry them on kitchen towels.

THE GARAM MASALA

2 To prepare the garam masala, heat a small frying pan and add all the ingredients. Dry-roast them for a few minutes on medium heat, till they release their natural oils and are intensely aromatic.

3 Transfer them to a heavy mortar or grinder and grind the spices to a fragrant, fine powder. Reserve.

THE TANDOORI PASTE

4 The next step is to prepare the tandoori paste or marinade. Put the ginger-garlic paste, red chilli-garlic paste, dried ginger powder, chaat masala powder, turmeric powder, salt and lime juice into a bowl. Add about 2–3 tsp of the freshly ground garam masala and the curd. Whisk the mixture really well, till it's a deep red colour and has the consistency of a semi-thick paste.

5 Taste the paste and check for a balance of flavours: it should be quite spicy and robust with the garlic, ginger, chillies and all the complex spices of the garam masala. It must have a deep red colour from the red chilli paste, with the lime juice giving it a nice tangy acidic finish. The curd softens the harshness of the spices slightly and gives the paste a creamy texture.

TO MARINATE THE CHICKEN

6 To marinate the chicken, use a sharp knife to make a couple of small gashes or slits on the surface of the pieces. Put the pieces into a large glass or plastic bowl and then add the tandoori paste to it.

7 Gently rub the rich, red tandoori paste into the chicken pieces, till they are thickly coated with the paste and a vivid red. Cover the bowl and put the chicken into the refrigerator to marinate for anywhere from 2 to 4 hours.

8 When the chicken is well marinated with the tandoori paste, remove it from the refrigerator and bring it to room temperature.

Ingredients

1 roasting chicken with skin (about 1¼ kg)	**THE TANDOORI PASTE**	**TO GRILL THE CHICKEN**

THE GARAM MASALA

- 1" cassia stick
- 1 tsp whole black peppercorns
- 2 brown cardamoms
- 4 green cardamoms
- 1½ tsp coriander seeds
- 1 tsp cumin seeds
- 4–5 cloves
- 1 bay leaf

THE TANDOORI PASTE

- 2 tbsp ginger-garlic paste
- 3 tbsp red chilli-garlic paste (see note)
- 2 tsp chaat masala
- 1 tsp dried ginger powder
- 1 tsp turmeric powder
- ¾ tsp salt
- Juice of 1 lime
- 3–4 tbsp whisked curd

TO GRILL THE CHICKEN

- 2 tbsp butter
- 1 tbsp ghee or olive oil

TO GARNISH

- Juice of 1 lime
- 2 tsp chopped fresh coriander leaves
- 2 onions, sliced in rings
- 4 lime wedges

TO GRILL THE CHICKEN

9 Pre-heat a gas, electric or charcoal grill, or even an oven's broiler or top griller, till its searing hot. It is essential that the grill be heated to its maximum temperature comparable to the interior of a tandoor and to give the chicken a charred, crisp exterior with a deliciously moist interior.

10 Once the grill or broiler is hot, grill the marinated chicken pieces 2"–3" away from the heat. Turn the pieces halfway through and baste them with the butter and ghee or olive oil every few minutes, till they are beautifully charred and crisp on the outside, while perfectly cooked and succulent on the inside.

11 The rich tandoori paste will form a thick charred crust as it cooks on the surface of the chicken; the skin protects the interior from drying out as it roasts to perfection in the high heat of the grill or oven.

12 After the chicken is cooked to perfection, remove it to a platter to rest for about 5 minutes. Sprinkle with lime juice to lift out all the wonderful smokiness of the chicken.

13 The chicken should be crisp and reddish on the outside while really juicy and full of flavour on the inside. The butter gives it a lovely, buttery, golden glaze along with the rich colour of the tandoori paste. The spices should be perfectly balanced with a slight acidic kick from the curd and lime coming through.

14 Garnish the tandoori chicken with coriander leaves, onion rings and lime wedges and serve straight away with mint chutney, naan and some pickled onions.

NOTE: Grind together 35 gms of dried red chillies, 3 garlic cloves and ¼ tsp of salt.

Chicken Recipes

Fish & Seafood
RECIPES

Maach Kalia
Pg 74

Grilled Surmai Steaks

4 SERVINGS

This grilled fish is perfect for an outdoor barbecue or even for lunch at home. Fresh dill and coriander form the base of the delicate and tangy marinade that turns these simple grilled steaks of fish into a real treat.

Ingredients

- 4½" thick large surmai or any firm-fleshed fish, cut into steaks
- ½ tsp refined oil
- Juice of 1 lime

THE MARINADE

- 4 garlic cloves
- 2 hot green chillies
- A generous handful of fresh dill leaves
- A handful of fresh coriander leaves and stems
- ½ tsp turmeric powder
- ½ tsp red chilli powder
- ½ tsp coriander powder
- ½ tsp salt
- ½ tsp refined oil
- 1 tbsp thick tamarind extract (see page 10)

Method

1. Put the fish on a plate or tray and drizzle the oil over them. Massage the steaks with the oil, till they are glossy all over.

THE MARINADE

2. To make the marinade, put the garlic, green chillies, dill leaves, coriander leaves, spice powders and salt into a heavy mortar or grinder and add the oil to lubricate the ingredients. Grind them to make a fresh green paste of a semi-fine consistency.

3. Put the paste into a small bowl and add the tamarind extract. Mix the two well, till the paste takes on a dark green colour and tastes really hot and tangy.

4. Spread the steaks out evenly on the plate and put 1–2 tsp of the paste on each steak. Gently massage the spicy, tangy marinade into the steaks, coating them evenly on both sides. Cover and leave the steaks to marinate at room temperature.

TO GRILL THE FISH

5. Preheat a grill or oven. Grill the fish a couple of inches away from the heat for 1–2 minutes on the first side, till it's a lovely golden colour. Carefully turn the steaks and grill them on the second side, till golden and cooked to perfection.

6. Test the fish by pressing on the flesh with a fork gently. The flesh should flake away easily from the central bone when pressed and should be evenly opaque all the way through. The total grilling time should be around 5–6 minutes; else the fish could overcook and dry out.

7. Once the fish is golden, crisp on the outside and cooked to perfection all the way through, remove the steaks to a platter, squeeze in some lime juice to lift the fresh, spice and tang of the marinade, with the delicate flavour of the fish coming through.

8. Serve the grilled fish steaks immediately and enjoy them with a fresh tomato or cucumber salad and a cold beverage.

Maach Kalia
(Bengali Fish in a Spicy Curd-Based Gravy)
6–8 SERVINGS

....

A wonderful fish curry usually made with any freshwater, firm fish. It owes its delicate taste to a combination of spices and curd, in a robust mustard oil base. Creamy, complex and absolutely exotic, this fish curry is a must try for every fish lover.

The Chakh le India Cookbook

Method

1 Clean the fish, remove and discard the skin and cut it into large curry-sized fillets. Wash well, drain and dry on kitchen towels.

THE MARINADE

2 Combine the marinade ingredients in a large bowl. Add the fish fillets and rub the yellowy paste into the fish gently, making sure all the pieces are coated with the spices. Cover and leave to marinate for about 15 minutes.

TO FRY THE FISH

3 To fry the marinated fish, heat 2 tbsp of mustard oil, till it smokes and then turn down the heat.

4 Add the fish pieces to the pan and fry them, till they are golden brown on both sides and about 70 per cent cooked. Remove the pan from the heat and leave the fish in it.

THE CURRY

5 To make the mustard oil-based curry base, heat the oil on high heat till it smokes, to burn off most of its bitterness. When it is almost clear in colour but still retains a hint of yellow, take the pan off the heat and let it cool slightly.

6 Return the pan to medium heat and add the red chillies, followed by the whole spices and bay leaf. Sauté them in the hot oil, till they crackle and are fragrant.

7 Add the onion and sauté, till it is a rich golden colour.

8 Throw in the green chillies and fry, till they soften slightly. Now add the ginger-garlic paste and sauté it for a couple of minutes, till it begins to turn light golden.

9 Sprinkle in the spice powders and sauté them on high heat to toast them, till they are intensely aromatic. Add a little water and deglaze the pan well, scraping up the rich pan juices on the base. Bhuno the masala with water repeatedly, till the aromatics and spices are homogenous and rich in colour, and the oil has risen to the surface.

10 Turn the heat down to low and gently stir in the whisked curd. Mix the curd and the masala, till the gravy takes on a yellowy-reddish colour and starts to bubble.

11 Add the salt and sugar to the simmering gravy and cook, till it is thick and reduced by about a third and the oil has surfaced, giving the curd gravy a mustard-yellow hue.

Ingredients

1 kg any freshwater firm-fleshed white fish	4 medium-hot dried red chillies	1 tsp coriander powder
2 tbsp mustard oil to fry the fish	½" cassia stick	500 gms whisked curd
THE MARINADE	½ tsp cumin seeds	1 tsp salt
½ tsp red chilli powder	3–4 cloves	A pinch of sugar
½ tsp turmeric powder	1 bay leaf	Juice of ½ a lime
½ tsp salt	1 onion, chopped fine	3–4 tsp chopped fresh coriander leaves
1 tsp refined oil	3 green chillies, split	
THE CURRY BASE	1 tbsp ginger-garlic paste	
2 tbsp mustard oil	¼ tsp turmeric powder	
	½ tsp hot red chilli powder	

12 Add the fried fish along with the fishy mustard oil in the pan and poach the fish gently to cook it through to perfection. Stir the kalia gently to combine everything and coat the fish in the spicy-sour curd gravy.

13 When the fish is cooked through and the gravy turns creamy rust in colour, with the mustard oil on its surface, squeeze in the lime juice to give the kalia an essential acidic kick, and sprinkle the chopped coriander leaves.

14 Turn off the heat and check for a balance of flavours: the fish should be cooked and taste creamy and tender having soaked up the spices and curd of the gravy. The curd gravy should be thick and semi-coating the fish. (It can be thinned down by adding a little water.) The kalia should have a brilliant rust colour, with the robust mustard oil and whole spices coming through. The curd should lend it a slight sourness and a creamy consistency while the sugar balances out the heat and sourness.

15 Serve with hot steamed rice.

Goan Prawn and Mango Ambotik

(Prawns in a Spicy Tangy Goan Masala with Ripe Mangoes)

6–7 SERVINGS

An exotic recipe from Goa, this dish brings together the magic of mangoes, coconut milk and the sour and pungent ambotik masala together with fresh prawns.

Method

1 First, peel the prawns and take off the heads. Leave the tails intact. Make a shallow cut down the spine of the prawns and remove the veins and discard them. Wash the prawns under cold running water and drain thoroughly.

THE AMBOTIK MASALA PASTE

2 To make the masala paste, heat a small frying pan. Add the oil and swirl the pan to coat it well. Now add the ginger and sauté on medium heat for a couple of minutes, till it is lightly coloured.

3 Now add the red chillies, whole spices and turmeric powder and sauté on medium heat, till they are aromatic. Turn off the heat, cool well and transfer to a blender. Grind to make a coarse paste.

4 Add the spring onions, tamarind extract and salt to the paste. Grind well, till the masala is of a fine consistency.

5 Taste to check for a balance of flavours: the masala should be really hot, and sour from the tamarind. Set aside.

THE CURRY

6 Peel and chop the mangoes. Reserve.

7 To make the base of the curry, heat the oil in a deep pan on medium to high heat. Add the ambotik masala paste with a few drops of water and fry well for a few minutes.

8 Once the oil surfaces and the spices are well cooked and a rich, deep brown colour, add the chopped mangoes. Cook covered, till the mangoes begin to disintegrate. Stir well to combine the ingredients.

9 Turn the heat down to a simmer and slowly add the coconut milk, stirring gently to combine with the mangoes and spices. Cover and simmer the curry for about 20 minutes or till the oil rises to the surface and the gravy is a rich deep yellow and light brown colour.

10 Now add the prawns and poach them in the simmering hot gravy for 5–7 minutes. Turn off the heat to allow the prawns to cook in the residual heat of the curry.

Ingredients

1 kg king-sized prawns

THE AMBOTIK MASALA PASTE

2 tsp refined oil

½" ginger

6–8 dried red Kashmiri chillies

6–8 dried red bor chillies

½ tsp cumin seeds

1 tsp coriander seeds

½ tsp fennel seeds

½ tsp whole black peppercorns

½ tsp turmeric powder

2 spring onions, white part only, chopped

3 tbsp tamarind extract (see page 10)

½–¾ tsp salt

THE CURRY BASE

3 ripe, sweet and slightly sour mangoes

2 tsp refined oil

3¼ cups thick coconut milk (see page 10)

½ tsp salt

THE TEMPERING

2 tsp refined oil

3 dried red Kashmiri chillies

A handful of chopped fresh coriander leaves

A handful of chopped spring onion greens

THE TEMPERING

11 To make the tempering, heat a small frying pan and add the oil. Add the remaining tempering ingredients and fry for a few minutes, till they are crisp.

12 Turn off the heat, cool the tempering for a couple of minutes and fold it into the prawn curry.

13 Check for a balance of flavours: the curry should be mildly sweet and sour, creamy and luscious in texture from the coconut milk, and slightly spicy from the hot ambotik masala.

14 Serve the curry with steamed rice, an onion salad, green chillies and chilled beer.

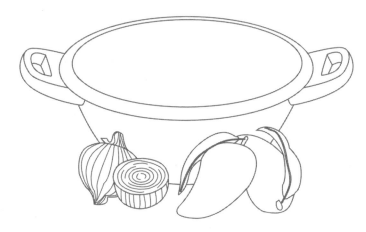

Goan Pomfret Reachado
(Pomfret Stuffed with a Spicy Goan Masala)
2 SERVINGS

. . . .

One of my favourite fried fish recipes of all times, this is indeed a fantastic Goan speciality. The reachado paste can be kept in a jar in the refrigerator and used for all kinds of meat and seafood recipes. It's really versatile and can transform any dish into a fiery-tangy beauty. It turns out best when the fish is fresh; and in case pomfret is unavailable, use any firm-fleshed white fish fillets.

Method

1 Clean and gut the fish and remove and discard the fins, tails and heads. Wash thoroughly, drain and dry on kitchen towels.

THE REACHADO MASALA PASTE

2 To make the reachado masala paste, heat a small frying pan and add all the paste ingredients except the vinegar and sugar. Dry-roast them on medium heat, till they are bursting with their natural aromas and oils.

3 Cool them a little and then transfer them to a spice grinder or blender. Add the vinegar and sugar, cover and grind well, adding a little more vinegar, if required, to keep the moisture for the paste intact, till the masala is really fine in its consistency.

4 Taste the paste. It should be fiery hot and pungent with the toddy vinegar and the wonderful warm spices. Set aside.

TO STUFF THE FISH

5 Now, to stuff the fish, take a sharp slim knife or a boning knife, and starting at the head end of the fish, cut through the flesh, sliding the tip of the blade against the central bone of the fish, to make a pocket down one side of the backbone almost up to the tail.

6 Repeat on the other side to make two deep pockets down each side of the fish's backbone. It is almost like removing the fillets completely so the same technique of filleting fish should work perfectly.

7 Take about 1 tbsp of the reachado masala paste and stuff it into each pocket between the rib, back bone and the thin, fleshy fillets. Smoothen the filling out with your fingers. Then season the fish with it and set aside, covered.

8 Repeat with the second fish.

TO COOK THE FISH

9 Heat a frying pan large enough to hold both the fish snugly and add a good ¼" layer of refined oil. Once it's hot, add 1 tbsp of butter and let it foam. When the foam subsides and the butter begins to get slightly nutty, add the stuffed pomfrets carefully.

10 As soon as they hit the pan, they will automatically sizzle. Fry them on medium to high heat for about 3–4 minutes and then carefully turn them over using a fish slice. Fry the fish on the second side for another 3–4 minutes and then turn the heat down. The skin of the fish will be crisp and turn golden brown as the sugars in the skin begin to caramelize.

Ingredients

2 medium-sized white pomfret

½ tsp salt

THE REACHADO MASALA PASTE

12 hot dried red chillies,
such as Byadagi

6–8 dried red Kashmiri chillies

6 garlic cloves

½" ginger

½ onion, quartered

1 tsp cumin seeds

½" cassia stick

6–8 cloves

½ tsp coriander seeds

½ tsp whole black
peppercorns

½ tsp turmeric powder

¼ tsp salt

2 tbsp Goan coconut
toddy vinegar (Dorelli's)

¼ tsp sugar

TO COOK THE FISH

Refined oil as required

2 tbsp butter

TO SERVE

Juice of ½ a lime

2 tsp chopped fresh
coriander leaves

---

11 Do not cover the pan as the steam will make the skin soggy. Fry the fish on low heat for a couple of minutes and check by gently pressing on the thickest part. If the flesh gives easily and flakes to the bone, it's cooked.

12 Once the fish is cooked, turn off the heat and add another tbsp of butter. Swirl the pan gently to coat the fish in the delicious buttery masala and pan juices.

13 Lift the fish out carefully and place them on a platter. Spoon the buttery pan juices on top, squeeze over the lime juice and sprinkle with coriander leaves.

14 Enjoy the steaming hot pomfret with a chilled beer.

machchi ke Sooley

(Rajasthani Baked Fish)

6 SERVINGS

Traditionally, these amazing fish kababs were cooked on a hot stone and therefore had a unique taste and flavour. Today however, they can be cooked on a grill or in the oven and are simple and quick to make. A must try!

Ingredients

1 kg rawas, kingfish or any white, firm-fleshed fish

THE MARINADE

3 tsp refined oil

10 garlic cloves, kept whole

2 medium-sized onions, sliced fine

½ tsp cumin seeds

1 tsp coriander seeds

½ tsp turmeric powder

½ tsp hot red chilli powder

½ tsp dried ginger powder

1 tsp dried mango powder

4 green chillies

3 tsp chopped fresh coriander leaves and stems

1 tsp salt

Juice of ½ a lime

1 tbsp melted ghee

TO BAKE

2 tsp butter

Juice of ½ a lime

2–3 tsp chopped fresh coriander leaves

Method

1 Cut the fish into 2" pieces. Wash and drain well. Dry the fish on kitchen towels, while preparing for the marinade.

THE MARINADE

2 First, heat the oil in a small frying pan and add the whole garlic cloves to it. Fry gently, till it turns a rich golden brown. Remove them to a plate and reserve.

3 Now add the finely sliced onions to the oil and fry them on medium to high heat, till they are a deep dark brown. Remove and drain on kitchen paper.

4 Put the fried garlic and onion into a heavy mortar or grinder.

5 Dry-roast the whole spices, spice powders, green chillies, coriander leaves and stems and salt on high heat, till slightly charred and very aromatic.

6 Add them to the mortar or grinder. Add the lime juice and ½ tbsp of melted ghee, and grind, till the masala paste is fine in consistency and deep golden brown. Add the remaining ½ tbsp of melted ghee to loosen the paste slightly.

7 Grease a medium-sized roasting tray with a little

ghee or butter and pre-heat an oven to 160ºC.

8 Place the fish in the tray, ½" apart and put a spoonful of the marinade on each piece.

9 Gently massage the marinade into the fish to coat the pieces completely. Dot each piece of fish with a small knob of butter, squeeze some lime juice on top and sprinkle with the coriander leaves.

10 Bake the fish in the oven at 160ºC for 12–14 minutes, turning the pieces over halfway through, till a toothpick inserted into the thickest part of a fish piece meets no resistance at all. Baste the fish periodically with the lovely rich roasting juices in the tray to glaze them beautifully.

11 Taste one small piece and check for a balance of flavours: the fish should be moist and meltingly soft in texture with the wonderfully robust complexity of the masala marinade coming through strongly. The fish should not be overpowered by the spices but heightened to perfection.

12 Serve the sooley on a platter with a tamarind and green chilli chutney.

The Chakh le India Cookbook

Mangalorean Prawn Curry

3–4 SERVINGS

I just love the simple but exotic flavours of India's west coast. This prawn curry is one of the easiest to make with coconut, aromatics and a few simple spices, and has a delicious tangy sweetish taste to it. Really easy and super good!

Ingredients

500 gms medium-sized prawns

2 tsp refined oil

THE MANGALOREAN MASALA PASTE

1 fresh coconut, grated

4–6 garlic cloves

½" ginger

6–8 hot dried red chillies

2 tbsp tamarind extract (see page 10)

¼ tsp grated jaggery

½ tsp turmeric powder

1 tsp salt

THE TEMPERING

2 tsp refined oil

½ tsp mustard seeds

¼ tsp fenugreek seeds

A few curry leaves

Method

1 First, peel the prawns and take off the heads. Leave the tails intact. Make a shallow cut down the spine of the prawns and remove the veins and discard them. Wash the prawns under cold running water and drain thoroughly.

THE MANGALOREAN MASALA PASTE

2 To make the masala paste, heat a small frying pan and dry-roast the grated coconut, garlic, ginger and red chillies, till they release their oils and are intensely aromatic.

3 Transfer them to a spice grinder and add the tamarind extract, jaggery, turmeric powder and salt. Grind all the ingredients to make a fine paste. Reserve.

THE CURRY

4 Heat a deep frying pan or sauté pan and add 2 tsp of refined oil. Swirl the pan to coat it well. Once the oil is hot, add the masala paste and bhuno on medium heat, using a little water, till the oil rises to the surface and the masala is rich brown and cooked through.

5 Add 1½ cups of water and stir to combine. Simmer the curry for 10–15 minutes to reduce and concentrate its flavours.

6 When it's reduced by about a third, add the prawns and poach them in the gently simmering curry for about 10 minutes so that they are cooked to perfection.

THE TEMPERING

7 While the prawns are being poached, quickly heat a metal ladle with 2 tsp of refined oil, add the tempering ingredients. Fry them, till they crackle and are aromatic and the curry leaves turn crisp.

8 Spoon the tempering into the curry, stir through and check for seasoning. Add some salt if needed.

9 Check for a balance of flavours: the curry should be tangy and mildly hot, and nutty sweet from the coconut, with the aromatics coming through on the finish. The prawns should have turned opaque and be fully curled, but not overcooked; they should be succulent on the inside.

10 Serve immediately with lemon or plain steamed rice.

Meen Kulambu

(Chettinad Fish Curry)

6–8 SERVINGS

....

A complex, spicy, tangy, sour fish curry that brings together all the textures of South India. This is an unusual curry, as it has several different layers of flavours and is deliciously soft when done. Use a meaty fish for best results.

The Chakh le India Cookbook

Method

1 Cut the fish into ½" thick steaks. Wash well, drain and dry on kitchen towels. Arrange the fish on a large plate or in a bowl.

THE MARINADE

2 Combine all the marinade ingredients in a small bowl. Mix well with a fork to make a smooth reddish yellow paste.

3 Put a little paste on each steak and then massage it in evenly, coating both sides. Cover and put into the refrigerator to marinate.

THE CHETTINAD MASALA PASTE

4 Now, to make the Chettinad masala paste, dry-roast all the ingredients except the oil in a small frying pan, till they release their natural oils and are intensely aromatic and fragrant.

5 Transfer them to a heavy mortar or grinder and add a little refined oil to lubricate the ingredients.

6 Grind the ingredients to a fine, deep reddish-brown paste. It should be really fine in its consistency. Set aside.

THE CURRY

7 Next, to make the base for the curry, heat a deep-sided pan. Add the oil and swirl the pan to coat it well. Now add the mustard seeds, fenugreek seeds and curry leaves and sauté them on medium heat, till they are crackling and nutty in aroma.

8 Add the shallots and sauté on medium heat, till they begin to change colour slightly and smell sweet and aromatic.

9 Mix in the ground Chettinad masala paste along with the thick tamarind extract.

10 Sauté the ingredients on high heat for a couple of minutes and then bhuno them with a little water, till the paste is a deep, dark brown and the oil rises to the surface. This is the base for the kulambu.

11 Now, add the thick and creamy coconut milk a little at a time, and stir it in gently, to prevent it from splitting. Season well with salt.

12 Turn the heat down and simmer the creamy, thick, brown gravy gently, making sure it does not boil (or the milk will split).

13 While the gravy is simmering and coming together, remove the fish from the refrigerator and bring it to room temperature.

14 Heat 2 tsp of refined oil in a large non-stick frying pan and fry the marinated fish steaks, till they are golden brown and crisp on both sides. Drain and set aside.

Ingredients

1 kg rawas or any white, firm-fleshed fish	1 tsp whole black peppercorns	½ tsp mustard seeds
2 tsp refined oil	4 cloves	¼ tsp fenugreek seeds
THE MARINADE	1 tsp coriander seeds	A few curry leaves
½ tsp turmeric powder	1 brown cardamom	6–8 shallots, julienned
¾ tsp red chilli powder	½" cassia stick	½ cup thick tamarind extract (see page 10)
A pinch of salt	1 tsp fennel seeds	2½ cups thick coconut milk (see page 10)
Juice of ½ a lime	5 hot dried red Guntur chillies	
2 tsp refined oil	4 dried red bor chillies	1 tsp salt
THE CHETTINAD MASALA PASTE	¼ tsp salt	**TO COMPLETE THE DISH**
6 garlic cloves	A little refined oil	3 tsp chopped fresh coriander leaves
1" ginger	**THE CURRY BASE**	Juice of ¾ of a lime
	2 tsp refined oil	

15 Once the gravy has simmered gently for 10–15 minutes and the oil has risen to the surface, add the fried fish steaks and poach them gently for about 10 minutes or till they are perfectly cooked and have absorbed all the complex flavours of the gravy.

16 As soon as the fish is tender and the curry is a deep, brownish crimson, turn off the heat.

17 Garnish the creamy textured gravy with coriander leaves and squeeze in the lime juice to give it a citrus tang.

18 Check for a balance of flavours: the fish should be cooked to perfection and firm in its texture. The creamy coconut milk-based gravy should be perfectly balanced with the complex heat of the masala paste, the sourness of the tamarind and the sweet creaminess of the rich coconut milk. The lime should lift the flavours of the finished curry.

19 Serve with hot steamed rice.

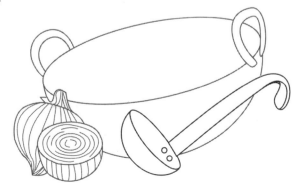

Chingdi Tarkari
(Bengali Prawn Curry)
4 SERVINGS

···

A deliciously simple Bengali prawn curry cooked with tradi-
tional spices, mustard oil and tomatoes. This light and semi-
thin prawn curry is an absolute winner and a great dish for
a dinner or luncheon.

The Chakh le India Cookbook

Method

1 First, peel the prawns and take off the heads and tails. Make a shallow cut down the spine of the prawns and remove the veins and discard them. Wash the prawns under cold running water and drain thoroughly.

THE MARINADE

2 Combine all the marinade ingredients in a large bowl. Add the prawns and rub the spices and oil into the prawns thoroughly, till they are evenly coated. Cover and set aside.

TO FRY THE PRAWNS

3 Now, to fry the prawns, heat 1 tbsp of mustard oil in a medium-sized non-stick frying pan and burn off some off its pungency, while keeping it yellow and robust in its aroma.

4 Add the marinated prawns to the pan and fry them on high heat, till they are beautifully browned all over and cooked through about 80 per cent. Turn off the heat and leave the prawns in the pan to rest.

THE CURRY

5 To make the base of the curry, put the mustard oil in a deep pan or kadhai on high heat till it smokes, to burn off its bitterness. Once the oil is almost clear and white in colour, take the pan off the heat and let it cool for a little while.

6 Return the pan to medium heat and add the five-spice mix, whole spices and bay leaf. Sauté them, till they are crackling and are fragrant.

7 Add the onion and sauté on medium heat, till it is soft and takes on a slight golden hue.

8 Add the ginger-garlic paste and sauté, till it begins to colour slightly.

9 Now add the spice powders and sauté on high heat so that they are well toasted. Sprinkle a little water and deglaze the pan, scraping up the rich pan deposits on the base.

10 Bhuno the masala with water repeatedly, till it is rich and homogenized, and the rust-coloured mustard oil rises to the surface.

11 Add the tomato and sauté it on medium heat, till it begins to soften a little and the base takes on a vibrant, reddish colour.

12 Once the aromatic and spice base is nicely cooked and well combined, add 3–4 cups of water to the pan. Stir the curry a few times to combine everything and simmer, till the oil surfaces again and the curry is perfectly cooked.

13 Add the salt and sugar to balance the acidity of the tomato.

Ingredients

500 gms medium-sized prawns	½" cassia stick	½ tsp sugar
1 tbsp mustard oil to fry the prawns	4 green cardamoms	Juice of ½ a lime
THE MARINADE	3 cloves	**THE GARNISH**
½ tsp turmeric powder	1 bay leaf	3–4 tsp chopped
½ tsp red chilli powder	1 onion, chopped fine	fresh coriander leaves
¾ tsp salt	3 tsp ginger-garlic paste	
2 tsp refined oil	1 tsp coriander powder	
THE CURRY BASE	1 tsp hot red chilli powder	
1 tbsp mustard oil	½ tsp turmeric powder	
1½ tsp Bengali five-spice mix (see note)	1 tomato, chopped fine	
	¾ tsp salt	

14 Immerse the prawns along with all their resting juices and oil into the simmering curry. Stir the prawns gently and poach them to a juicy tenderness for about 6–8 minutes.

15 Simmer the curry uncovered to reduce it a little.

16 Then turn off the heat and squeeze in some lime juice to lift the curry and prawns. Sprinkle the coriander leaves for a contrast of colour.

17 Check for a balance of flavours: this simple, semi-thin curry should be wonderfully robust with the taste of the mustard oil and whole spices coming through; the spicy tomato-based curry perfectly balanced with a delicious spicy, sweet and sour character. The prawns should be very tender and juicy, having absorbed all the flavours of the curry as well as the mustard oil in which they were fried earlier. Finally, the lime juice should lift the whole curry perfectly.

18 Serve with steamed rice.

NOTE: Bengali five-spice mix or panch phoran comprises a mix of equal quantities of cumin seeds, mustard seeds, fenugreek seeds, nigella seeds and fennel seeds.

Chettinad Fish Fry

4–5 SERVINGS

A favourite from the Chettinad region of Tamil Nadu, this is a deliciously spicy and tangy fried fish that is quick and easy to make. It also makes a great party dish! Store any leftover marinade in the refrigerator and use it to add a lovely complex flavour to any other curried dish.

Ingredients

750 gms any firm-fleshed white fish

THE CHETTINAD MASALA PASTE

6 garlic cloves

½" ginger

½ tsp cumin seeds

1 tsp fennel seeds

1 tsp coriander seeds

½ tsp whole black peppercorns

½ tsp mustard seeds

A small handful of curry leaves

¾ tsp salt

3 tsp refined oil

1 tomato, chopped fine

2 tbsp thick tamarind extract (see page 10)

½ tsp turmeric powder

1 tsp hot red chilli powder

TO FRY THE FISH

3 tsp refined oil

¾ tsp salt

A knob of butter

THE GARNISH

Juice of 1 lime

3–4 tsp chopped fresh coriander leaves

Method

1 Skin the fish and fillet it. Cut it into medium-sized chunks. Wash well, drain and gently pat dry with kitchen paper. Transfer the pieces on to a large platter or tray, cover and set aside.

THE CHETTINAD MASALA PASTE

2 To make the Chettinad masala paste, heat a small frying pan and add the aromatics, whole spices and curry leaves. Dry-roast them, till they begin to change colour, release their natural oils and are wonderfully aromatic.

3 Transfer them to a heavy mortar or grinder. Add the salt, oil and a little water. Grind the ingredients, till it's a fine, peppery, dark brown paste.

4 Add the tomato, tamarind extract, turmeric powder and chilli powder and grind, till the tomatoes have completely disintegrated and the paste is thick, deep and dark brown.

5 The paste should be peppery hot, complex and tangy with the tomatoes and tamarind balancing out the intense heat of the pepper and spices.

6 Mix the masala paste a few times to combine everything well, and add a little salt or tamarind to balance the spices if required.

7 Smear each piece of fish with the thick masala paste, making sure they are evenly and gently coated in the tangy, hot paste.

8 Cover the fish and leave to marinate for 15 minutes.

TO FRY THE FISH

9 To fry the fish, heat the oil in a medium-sized non-stick pan. When the oil is hot, season the fish with salt and put the pieces in batches into the hot oil. Fry the pieces for 1–2 minutes on one side to give them a delicious, golden spice crust. Turn the pieces over carefully and fry the second side, till golden and crisp. Add a little butter for flavour and colour.

10 Test the fish by pressing the flesh with a fork: if it flakes easily, it is cooked. Remove the fish from the pan and drain the excess oil on kitchen paper.

11 Now, squeeze some lime juice over the fish and garnish with coriander leaves.

12 Serve this delicious, spicy and tangy, Chettinad fish fry straight away.

Chingdi Tarkari
Pg 84

Machchi ke Sooley
Pg 80

Malabari Prawn Curry
Pg 102

Chettinad Fish Fry
Pg 86

Mustard Prawns

4–5 SERVINGS

These butch-flavoured prawns are a clinch to make. The Bengali marinade plays a perfect partner to the sweetness of the prawns. Quick and simple to prepare, the prawns have to be marinated for a while and they are good to go. A must try and a great dinner party dish!!

Ingredients

750 gms king-sized prawns (shelled, de-veined and washed)

THE ROBUST MARINADE

¼" ginger

3 hot green chillies

1 tsp fennel seeds

½ tsp coriander seeds

½ tsp whole white peppercorns

½ tsp salt

2 tbsp kasundi or Indian mustard paste or any sharp, grainy mustard

½ tsp red chilli powder

2 tsp mustard oil

Juice of 1 lime

TO COMPLETE THE DISH

Juice of ½ a lime

¼ cup of fresh dill leaves

Method

1 Peel the prawns and take off the heads and tails. Make a shallow cut down the spine of the prawns and remove the veins and discard them. Wash the prawns under cold running water and drain thoroughly.

THE MARINADE

2 The next step is to prepare the marinade. Dry-roast the ginger, green chillies and whole spices, till they release their natural oils and are intensely fragrant. Transfer them to a heavy mortar or grinder, add the salt and a little water and grind them to make a fine paste.

3 Add the kasundi, chilli powder, mustard oil and lime juice to the paste and mix it well with a fork, till it is smooth in consistency and has a sharp aroma. Put the prawns into a glass bowl and add the mustard marinade to it.

4 Rub the marinade into the prawns gently with your hands, till all the prawns are evenly coated with the sharp, delicately spiced marinade. Cover the prawns and leave to marinate for about 15 minutes.

TO COOK THE PRAWNS

5 Preheat an oven to 160ºC.

6 Put the prawns into a medium-sized roasting tray, spread them out evenly in one layer and put them into the oven to roast for 8–10 minutes or till the prawns are perfectly cooked through and curled up nicely. They should be opaque and firm to the touch.

7 Turn off the oven and let the prawns roast for a minute or two to cook them through completely.

8 Take the golden prawns out of the oven and arrange them on an attractive serving platter.

TO SERVE

9 Squeeze the lime juice over the prawns to jazz up the flavours and scatter the delicate dill leaves on top.

10 Serve these scrumptious, Bengali mustard prawns immediately.

Doi Maach
(Bengali Fish in a Spiced Curd Gravy)
6–8 SERVINGS

Bengal undoubtedly has some of the best fish curry recipes but this one is more special than the others. It brings together some meaty, freshwater fish with the butch and robust flavours of mustard oil and whole spices and then balances them perfectly with delicately sour curd to give the dish a delicious and refined effect.

Method

1 Cut the fish into steaks, wash well, drain and dry on kitchen towels.

THE MARINADE

2 Combine all the dry marinade ingredients in a large bowl. Mix in the mustard oil to help the spices stick to the fish and mix well. Add the fish and gently massage the marinade into the pieces. Cover and set aside to marinate for about 15 minutes.

TO FRY THE FISH

3 To fry the fish, put a medium-sized frying pan on high heat and add 2 tbsp of mustard oil. Heat the oil till it smokes, to burn off its bitterness. Once hot, add the marinated fish pieces and fry them for a couple of minutes on each side on medium heat, till they are a golden brown around the edges and richly coloured. After the fish is almost 75 per cent cooked, remove on to a plate and set aside.

THE CURRY

4 To make the curry, reheat the same pan with the fishy mustard oil and after adding the whole spices and bay leaf, sauté them on medium heat, till they are fragrant and change colour.

5 Add the puréed onion and sauté, till it turns a light golden brown. Add the ginger-garlic paste and bhuno the aromatic spice base with little water, till it's a rich, light golden colour and the oil rises to the surface.

6 Now, whisk the curd well in a bowl. Add the turmeric powder and chilli powder and mix well.

7 Turn the heat down to medium-low and add the whisked curd and spice mixture to the pan. Stir gently and simmer for 10–15 minutes, or till the oil surfaces and the gravy is a golden mustard colour.

8 Sprinkle in the salt and stir through to combine well.

Ingredients

1 kg rohu, rawas or any freshwater fish	½ tsp cumin seeds
2 tbsp mustard oil to fry the fish	1 bay leaf
THE MARINADE	1 onion, puréed
½ tsp turmeric powder	2 tsp ginger-garlic paste
¾ tsp red chilli powder	500 gms whisked curd
¾ tsp salt	½ tsp turmeric powder
1 tsp mustard oil	1 tsp medium-hot red chilli powder
THE CURRY BASE	¾ tsp salt
½" cassia stick	Juice of 1 lime
4 cloves	
4–5 green cardamoms	

9 Add the fried fish, along with all the resting juices in the plate and simmer it for another 10 minutes to gently poach the fish to perfection.

10 When the oil rises to the surface and the fish is cooked perfectly, turn off the heat.

11 Check for a balance of flavours: the curry should be robust, slightly spicy and delicately sour with the curd and spices. The fish should be tender and soft, having absorbed the wonderful flavours of the curry as it cooks to perfection.

12 Squeeze the lime juice to add a citrus kick for a lovely contrast.

13 Serve the doi maach with hot steamed rice.

Pan-Seared Grouper with Mustard Cream Sauce

1–2 SERVINGS

....

This dish is perfect as the main course for a formal sit-down dinner. It may appear complicated at a first glance, but it is actually really simple. Timing is of the essence while making this dish, so prepare the sauce in advance, finish the vegetables and fry the fish last. Then just put it all together for a posh, French, fine dining meal with a South Indian tinge, as this is typical Puducherry cuisine.

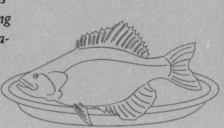

Method

1 Cut the fillets and leave the skin on. Trim and remove the pin bones (the ones holding the fins to the ribcage). Wash the fillets and drain thoroughly. Set aside.

THE VEGETABLES

2 Next, blanch the vegetables. Bring some water to a boil in a deep pan and add the salt. Add the carrots and blanch for 8–10 minutes or till they are slightly tender. Take care not to overcook the carrots.

3 Fish them out with a slotted spoon and transfer to a chilled water bath to refresh them; this ensures that their colour remains intact and they do not become more tender than required. Set aside.

4 Now add the beans to the same boiling water and blanch them on a rolling boil for 3–4 minutes, or till they are just slightly softened, but still very firm. Remove, refresh and keep them aside with the carrots.

THE SAUCE

5 To make the sauce, heat a small pan and add a drop of ghee. Swirl the pan and then add the butter. When the butter is hot, add the shallots and sauté on medium heat, till they caramelize and turn light golden.

6 Add the cream, mustard, lime juice, salt and pepper and stir on low heat to combine well. Simmer the sauce for a few minutes.

7 Add the chopped parsley and a little water and mix well. Simmer the smooth mustard cream sauce for a couple of minutes longer. Turn off the heat and cover the pan. Keep warm.

TO FRY THE FISH

8 Now to fry the fish, put the ghee in a heavy, non-stick frying pan on high heat. Season the fish fillets with salt and pepper and squeeze in some lime juice. Put the fillets in the pan, skin side down, and press down on them gently to sear and create a rich caramelized crust on the skin.

9 Now lower the heat slightly and fry the fish, till a thick rich brown crust appears on the underside of the fillets. Turn off the heat and turn the fillet over to complete the cooking in the pan's residual heat.

10 Add a little butter and swirl the pan to coat and colour the fillets beautifully.

TO COMPLETE THE DISH

11 Put the blanched vegetables into a sauté pan on medium heat. Add the butter, squeeze in the lime

Ingredients

2 medium-sized fillets of grouper

THE VEGETABLES

2 carrots, cut into
  medium-sized batons

A handful of French beans

1 tsp salt

THE SAUCE

1/8 tsp ghee

2 tsp butter

8–10 shallots, julienned

½ cup light cream

2–3 tsp kasundi or
  regular grainy mustard

Juice of 1 lime

¼ tsp salt

¼ tsp freshly ground black pepper

3 tsp chopped fresh parsley

THE TEMPERING

2 tsp butter

1 tsp ghee

4 dried red chillies

½ tsp mustard seeds

TO COOK

Ghee to shallow-fry the fish

¼ tsp salt

½ tsp freshly ground black pepper

Juice of ½ a lime

2 tsp butter

TO COMPLETE THE DISH

1 tsp butter

Juice of ½ a lime

¼ tsp salt

¼ tsp freshly ground black pepper

juice and season well with the salt and pepper. Cook and toss the vegetables to coat them with a lemon butter dressing.

12 Check that the fish is completely cooked, by inserting a toothpick into the thickest part of the fillet: it should go in without any resistance.

13 Arrange half the vegetables on one side of an attractive white plate.

14 Carefully lift out a fillet and place it in the centre of the plate, then place the second one over it to form an X on the plate.

15 Arrange the remaining vegetables on the other side of the fish.

16 Spoon a little mustard cream sauce over the fish and let it rest for a minute while the tempering is prepared on the side with the red chillies and mustard seeds fried in hot butter and ghee.

17 Spoon the hot tempering with the butter and ghee over the fish and serve with lime wedges on the side.

Punjabi Methiwali Machchi

(Punjabi Fenugreek Fish)

6–8 SERVINGS

. . . .

The city of Amritsar in Punjab absolutely loves fried fish and this recipe is a truly, rustic Punjabi dish that brings together all the flavours of the region perfectly. Ideally, this works best with meaty freshwater fish which makes all the difference to the taste.

Method

1 Skin the fish and cut it into medium-sized fillets. Wash well, drain and dry on kitchen towels.

2 Wash the spinach and fenugreek leaves in several changes of water. Boil them in a little water, till they are fully cooked. Turn off the heat and leave to cool.

THE MARINADE

3 Combine the marinade ingredients in a small bowl. Pour it over the fish and mix well to ensure that the fish is well coated in the marinade. Cover and place in the refrigerator to marinate.

TO FRY THE FISH

4 Remove the fish from the refrigerator and bring to room temperature.

5 Heat the oil in a hot frying pan and fry the fish in batches on high heat, till the fillets are light golden brown around the edges. Remove and drain on kitchen paper. Keep warm.

THE CURRY

6 To make the curry base of the dish, heat a large frying pan and add 1 tbsp of the oil in which the fish was fried. Add the ginger and garlic and sauté on medium heat, till they begin to colour slightly. Add the onion and continue to sauté, till it turns a light, nutty, golden brown.

7 Now add the spice powders and bhuno for a minute to toast them well. Add a little water to deglaze and amalgamate the spices and aromatics. Bhuno, till the masala is a rich reddish, yellowy, light brown.

8 Pour in the tomato purée and turn the heat down to low. Simmer the ingredients, stirring periodically, till the purée is a rich red and the oil rises to the surface.

9 Stir in the salt and sugar to balance the acidity of the tomatoes. Mix well.

10 Sprinkle in a little water if the gravy thickens too much and continue to simmer.

11 Chop the boiled spinach and fenugreek leaves fine, and add them to the simmering curry, stirring to mix well. Gently cook the greens and the rich, spiced tomato gravy for a few minutes to combine everything.

Ingredients

1 kg freshwater sole or rawas	**THE CURRY BASE**	1 kg ripe tomatoes, puréed
3 tbsp refined oil to fry the fish	½" ginger, chopped fine	½ tsp salt
2–3 cups fresh spinach leaves	6 garlic cloves, chopped fine	A pinch of sugar
2 cups fresh fenugreek leaves	1 medium-sized onion, julienned	A dollop of butter
THE MARINADE	½ tsp cumin powder	Juice of ½ a lime
Juice of 1 lime	½ tsp turmeric powder	
½ tsp salt	½ tsp coriander powder	
½ tsp freshly ground white pepper	½ tsp medium-hot red chilli powder	

12 Finally add the fried fish and move them around gently to ensure they are fully coated in the thick gravy. Continue to simmer for about 10 minutes to cook the fish to perfection and concentrate the gravy.

13 Check for a balance of flavours: the gravy should be thick in its consistency, and should coat the fish properly while taking on some of its flavours. It should be delicately spiced and bursting with the intense concentrated tomatoes with the delicate, mild bitterness of the leafy vegetables coming through.

14 Add a dollop of butter to make it really special and also squeeze in some lime juice if desired.

15 Serve hot to warm, with parantha.

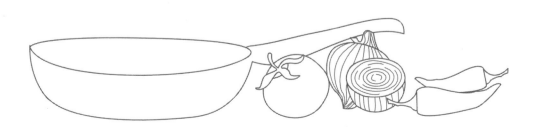

Andhra Chepa Pulusu
(Tangy Andhra Fish Curry)
6–7 SERVINGS

This is my version of a wonderfully tangy and hot fish curry from Andhra Pradesh. Essentially made with rohu which is a delicious and meaty freshwater fish, it also tastes wonderful with any other firm-fleshed fish.

Method

1 Clean the fish and cut it into medium-sized pieces with the skin. Wash well, drain and dry on kitchen towels.

THE MARINADE

2 Combine all the dry marinade ingredients in a small bowl. Add the oil and mix to make a fine paste. Rub the marinade into the fish, massaging it in well. Cover and put into the refrigerator for 15–20 minutes.

THE GARAM MASALA

3 Dry-roast the garam masala ingredients in a small frying pan on medium heat. Transfer to a mortar or grinder and grind to make a fine powder. Set aside.

THE ONION-CHILLI PASTE

4 Put the chopped onions and green chillies into a spice grinder and grind to make a semi-fine paste. Reserve.

THE CURRY

5 Remove the marinated fish from the refrigerator and bring to room temperature.

6 Heat a medium-sized frying pan and add the sesame oil. Swirl the pan to coat it well. When the oil is hot, add the fish and fry, till it is light brown and a nice caramelized crust forms on all sides. Remove the pieces and drain on kitchen paper.

7 Add the mustard seeds, fenugreek seeds and curry leaves to the same pan containing the oil and fish juices. Sauté for a few minutes on medium heat, till they begin to crackle and release their aromas.

8 Add the onion-chilli paste and sauté for a few minutes, till it turns light brown.

9 Next, add the freshly ground garam masala and continue sautéing on medium heat, till the base of the curry is a rich golden brown and the oil rises to the surface—a clear sign that the spices are well cooked.

10 Add the tomato purée and stir through. Follow it up with the tamarind extract, jaggery and salt. Simmer the gravy for 10–15 minutes, till the oil rises to the surface and the curry is nice and thick and reduced by about a third.

11 Pour in 1 cup of water and mix well. Cook the gravy on low heat for 10–15 minutes longer, to amalgamate the flavours. The curry should be a rich, brownish-red colour and the oil should have risen to the surface.

Ingredients

1 kg rohu	3 green cardamoms	3–4 tbsp tamarind extract (see page 10)
THE MARINADE	4–5 cloves	¼ tsp grated jaggery
1 tbsp ginger-garlic paste	**THE ONION-CHILLI PASTE**	1 tsp salt
1 tsp turmeric powder	2 onions, chopped coarsely	**THE GARNISH**
1 tsp red chilli powder	4–5 hot green chillies	3–4 tsp chopped fresh coriander leaves
1 tsp salt	**THE CURRY BASE**	
1 tsp coriander powder	2 tbsp sesame oil	
½ tsp cumin powder	1 tsp mustard seeds	
1 tsp sesame oil	½ tsp fenugreek seeds	
THE GARAM MASALA	A few curry leaves	
1" cassia stick	1 cup fresh tomato purée	

12 Add the fried fish to the curry and poach for 10–12 minutes, or till the fish is fully cooked and flakes easily with a fork.

13 Check for a balance of flavours: the curry should be mildly spicy, aromatic and sour from the tamarind extract. The fish in turn, should be tender and moist.

14 Turn off the heat, leave for a few minutes for the curry to mature and sprinkle the chopped coriander leaves.

15 Serve with hot steamed rice.

NOTE: Frying the fish first in hot oil before adding it to a curry intensifies its taste and makes for a richer and more robust curry.

Konkani Jhinga Masala
(Konkani Masala Prawns)
6–7 SERVINGS

. . . .

A quintessential sample of India's west coast! The fresh coastal flavours are irresistible as they are beautifully spiced with the unique sweet and sour taste of kokum and jaggery.

The Chakh le India Cookbook

Method

1 First, peel the prawns and take off the heads, reserving them for a lovely prawn stock. Leave the tails intact. Make a shallow cut down the spine of the prawns and remove the veins and discard them. Wash the prawns under cold running water and drain thoroughly. Cover them and set aside.

THE HOT KONKANI MASALA PASTE

2 To make the masala paste, heat the oil in a medium-sized frying pan. Add the masala paste ingredients and fry them on medium heat, till they release their natural oils and are aromatic.

3 Once the ingredients are fried, turn off the heat and transfer the sizzling hot ingredients to a heavy mortar or grinder. Grind them to a semi-coarse, yellow-green paste. Set aside.

THE CURRY

4 Now for the base. Heat the oil in a heavy frying pan. Add the onion and sauté on medium heat, till light golden with a nutty sweet aroma.

5 Add the fresh masala paste to the pan and sauté for a couple of minutes on high heat to fry well. Turn the heat down slightly and add the kokum extract and jaggery to the pan. Stir in gently to combine well.

6 Bhuno this aromatic spice base repeatedly with water on high heat, till the base is perfectly homogenous and the oil begins to rise to the surface—a clear sign that the spices are fully cooked.

7 Add the prawns and season them well with salt. Toss the prawns in the sweet-sour masala to coat them in the gravy.

8 Cover the pan and let the prawns cook in the steam for 4–5 minutes or till they are firm and opaque and have taken on the delicate lemon-yellow colour of the masala.

9 Uncover the pan and turn up the heat to reduce the thick masala.

10 Turn off the heat and squeeze in the lime juice. Sprinkle the coriander leaves for a lovely herby freshness.

11 Check for a balance of flavours: the prawns should be perfectly cooked, really juicy and delicately

Ingredients

1 kg medium-sized prawns	½ tsp whole white peppercorns	3 tsp kokum extract (see page 10)
THE HOT KONKANI MASALA PASTE	½ tsp turmeric powder	A little grated jaggery to balance the sourness of the kokum
2 tsp refined oil	¾ tsp medium-hot red chilli powder	½ tsp salt
1 large cup freshly grated coconut	1/3 cup chopped fresh coriander leaves and stems	Juice of ½ a lime
4 hot green chillies	½ tsp salt	**THE GARNISH**
1" ginger	**THE CURRY BASE**	3–4 tsp chopped fresh coriander leaves
½" cassia stick	2 tsp refined oil	
1 tsp coriander seeds	½ an onion, julienned	

infused with the spicy, sweet and sour, nutty, green-yellow Konkani masala paste. The thick masala should completely coat the prawns and provide an intense, reduced and concentrated dry gravy that complements the fresh prawns to perfection.

12 Serve these deliciously fresh, west coast prawns straight away with roti or bread.

Konkani Hara Masala Pomplet
(Konkani Pomfret with Fresh Herbs)
2–4 SERVINGS

This west coast Indian dish is really quick and simple; a combination of the nutty fresh sweetness of coconut and the fresh herbs make for a perfect creation with the delicate flavour of the pomfret thrown in. It can also be baked in an oven with a little butter and lime juice squeezed in.

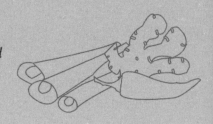

Method

1 Clean the fish and cut it into ½" thick steaks. Wash thoroughly, drain and dry on kitchen paper.

THE MARINADE

2 Combine all the marinade ingredients in a bowl and mix well to make a wet paste. Add the pomfret steaks and rub the marinade into the fish well. Cover with cling wrap and keep in the refrigerator to marinate while you make the Konkani hara masala.

THE KONKANI HARA MASALA

3 To make the hara masala, heat a small frying pan. Add all the masala ingredients, except the kokum extract and salt, and dry-roast them for a few minutes, till they release their wonderful aroma and natural oils.

4 Transfer them to a spice grinder and add the kokum extract, which will lend a nice Konkani tang to the masala paste. Grind, till the paste has a fine consistency, adding a little water if necessary. Season with salt and grind once more, till well combined. Set aside.

5 Remove the pomfret steaks from the refrigerator and add the masala paste. Mix well ensuring that the steaks are well covered with the masala. Cover and leave to marinate for 15 minutes at room temperature.

TO FRY THE FISH

6 Now, to shallow-fry our steaks. Take a non-stick frying pan that is large enough to hold all the steaks and leave it on medium to high heat, till hot. Add enough oil to come halfway up the thickness of the fish steaks.

7 Once the oil is hot, add the steaks and fry them in the hot oil without moving them around, in order to set the masala on the steaks.

8 Fry the first side, till it is light golden brown with a crisp spice crust. Carefully turn them over and fry the second side, till beautifully golden and crisp.

9 Check to see if the fish is cooked by gently pressing on the steaks, the fish should begin to flake easily

Ingredients

1 large white pomfret	4–5 garlic cloves	**THE GARNISH**
Refined oil for shallow-frying the fish	¼" ginger	1 onion, sliced
THE MARINADE	3 triphal pods (see note)	3–4 lime wedges
½ tsp turmeric powder	½ tsp cumin seeds	2 tsp chopped fresh coriander leaves
1 tsp red chilli powder	¼ cup chopped fresh coriander leaves	
½ tsp salt	2 tsp kokum extract (see page 10)	
1 tsp refined oil	½ tsp salt	
THE KONKANI HARA MASALA		
½ a coconut, grated		
4 medium-hot green chillies		

when pressed lightly. Another method of checking for doneness is to insert a toothpick into them. If it goes through the fish without any resistance, the fish is cooked.

10 Transfer the fish to a platter lined with kitchen paper or tissue to absorb the excess oil.

11 Turn out on to an attractive serving platter.

12 Garnish with the onion slices and lime wedges and scatter the coriander leaves on top.

13 Serve warm with a cold drink and enjoy the wonderfully simple and flavoursome Konkani dish as a heavy starter or as part of a meal as a dry main course.

NOTE: Triphal pods are also called Goa spiceberries.

Malabari Prawn Curry

4–5 SERVINGS

....

One of my all-time favourites, this prawn curry both looks and tastes amazing. Cook it the next time you're having someone over and they will be left spellbound by this simple, yet exotic curry. Simply superb!

Method

1 First, peel the prawns and take off the heads. Leave the tails intact. Make a shallow cut down the spine of the prawns and remove the veins and discard them. Wash the prawns under cold running water and drain thoroughly.

THE MARINADE

2 Combine the marinade ingredients in a bowl. Add the prawns, rub the marinade into them, making sure that all of them are evenly coated in the simple marinade. Cover and put into the refrigerator.

THE CURRY

3 To make the base, heat a medium-sized pan and add the oil. Once the oil is hot and nutty in its aroma, add the mustard seeds and sauté them on medium heat, till they crackle.

4 Add the green chillies, curry leaves, shallots, ginger and garlic. Sauté them on medium heat for a few minutes, till they are soft, fragrant and slightly coloured.

5 Sprinkle in the spice powders and salt and sauté the spices for a few minutes, till well toasted and intensely aromatic.

6 Add a few drops of water and bhuno the spices and aromatics a few times on high heat, till the masala is homogenous and the oil has risen to the surface. Once the masala is a rich yellow-green in colour and fully cooked, turn the heat down to low and add the coconut milk to the pan.

7 Stir the coconut milk and spice base and bring to a gentle boil to amalgamate the flavours.

8 Turn the heat down further and simmer the delicate, golden-coloured curry, till it is reduced by a quarter, is semi-thick in consistency and a little oil has risen to the surface.

9 Now add the cherry tomatoes and simmer them in the coconut milk gravy for 6–8 minutes or till they have softened a little and released some of their sweetness into the gravy.

10 Stir everything together a few times and then add the prawns and coconut cream to the simmering gravy.

11 Gently stir the prawns around and poach them in the delicate curry, till they are perfectly cooked through and succulent. The prawns are ready to eat when they curl up fully and are firm to the touch.

Ingredients

750 gms large prawns	2–3 green chillies, slit	2½ cups fresh coconut milk (see page 10)
THE MARINADE	A few curry leaves	
½ tsp turmeric powder	4–5 shallots, julienned	10 cherry tomatoes, halved
½ tsp red chilli powder	½" ginger, sliced thin	¾ cup thick coconut cream (commercial)
½ tsp salt	4–5 garlic cloves, sliced thin	
2 tsp refined oil	½ tsp turmeric powder	Juice of ½ a lime
THE CURRY BASE	½ tsp red chilli powder	2 tsp chopped fresh coriander leaves
3 tsp refined or coconut oil	½ tsp coriander powder	
½ tsp mustard seeds	½ tsp salt	

12 Now, add the lime juice to the pan and stir through, then sprinkle the coriander leaves and turn off the heat.

13 Check for a balance of flavours: the prawns should be thoroughly cooked, moist from within, tender and beautifully flavoured with the delicate coconut and spice-based gravy. The lovely, bright yellow curry should be creamy, with the rich coconut sweetness and the delicate spices coming through perfectly on the finish. The cherry tomatoes and coriander leaves should provide a distinct flourish and an amazing contrast of colours as well.

14 Serve with steamed or lemon rice.

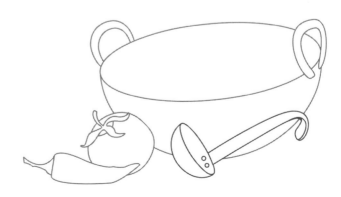

Vegetarian
RECIPES

Aamras ki Kadhi
Pg 107

Aamras ki Kadhi
(Mango Curry)

6–8 SERVINGS

. . . .

This is another of my favourite recipes. The sweet and sour flavour of the mangoes turns this simple kadhi into something completely exotic, and they make perfect partners to the robust flavours of the mustard and chillies. Another great example of the many ways mangoes are used in India. Fantastic!

Ingredients

- 1 large cup aamras or pulpy, ripe mango purée
- 1 cup raw, green mango purée
- 1½ cups curd whisked with 1½ cups water
- ¼ tsp turmeric powder
- ¼ tsp mild red chilli powder
- 1 tsp salt

THE KADHI BASE

- 2 tsp refined oil
- ½ tsp cumin seeds
- ¼ tsp fenugreek seeds
- ½ tsp mustard seeds
- A few curry leaves
- A pinch of asafoetida powder
- 3 green chillies, split
- 3 tbsp boondi or gram flour drops

THE TEMPERING

- 1 tsp refined oil
- ¼" ginger, julienned
- 2 dried red Kashmiri chillies, broken or cut fine
- 2 tsp fresh coriander leaves
- 1 tbsp boondi

Method

1 Put the ripe and green mango purées in a large bowl, along with the diluted curd and spice powders. Mix them together really well, till full blended. Set aside.

2 Heat the oil for the kadhi in a wok or kadhai and add the whole spices, curry leaves, asafoetida powder and green chillies. Sauté on medium heat, till they crackle and are intensely aromatic.

3 Turn the heat down and then add the mango and curd mixture to the pan, stirring continuously to prevent the curd from splitting.

4 Sprinkle in the salt.

5 Cook the kadhi on low heat for about 15 minutes, adding a little more diluted curd if the mixture becomes too thick, owing to the raw mango purée. Add the boondi and mix them in well. The boondi will absorb the kadhi and become soft, while the starch in the boondi will thicken the kadhi slightly. Simmer the kadhi, stirring it gently, till it's thin and perfectly cooked.

6 Once the kadhi is cooked, the oil rises to the surface and the aroma of raw spices disappears, turn off the heat and put the kadhi into a serving bowl.

7 Heat the oil for the tempering in a small frying pan and add the tempering ingredients. Fry them in the hot oil, till crisped and fragrant.

8 Pour the tempering over the kadhi.

9 Check for a balance of flavours: the kadhi should be creamy and mango-flavoured, with the slight sourness of the curd and raw mango coming through and just a delicate hint of the whole spices. The first tempering should give it a lift of flavour and provide a great textural and visual contrast to the lemony yellow of the aamras kadhi.

10 Serve with hot puri.

Aloo ke Gutke
(Mustard-Flavoured Potatoes)

4–5 SERVINGS

This recipe is a Kumaon take on cumin potatoes. It's really simple and quick to make and the robust flavours of the mustard oil and crisp red chilli and coriander tempering really make the flavours of the potatoes and spices shine beautifully.

Ingredients

4–5 potatoes

3 tbsp mustard oil

1 tsp medium-hot red chilli powder

1 tsp coriander powder

½ tsp turmeric powder

A pinch of asafoetida powder

1 tsp cumin seeds

½ tsp salt

THE TEMPERING

1 tbsp mustard oil

3 hot dried red chillies

2–4 tsp chopped fresh coriander leaves

Juice of ½ a lime

Method

1 Scrub the potatoes and par-boil them, till almost cooked. Peel and leave to cool slightly. Then cube them into medium to small sizes. Set aside.

2 Heat a medium-sized frying pan or kadhai and add the mustard oil. Heat the mustard oil on high heat till it smokes, to burn off its bitterness. Once the oil is almost clear in colour, take the pan off the heat and let it cool for a couple of minutes.

3 In the meantime, mix the chilli, coriander and turmeric powders in a small bowl. Add just enough water to form a semi-thick masala paste. Set aside.

4 Now, return the pan with the cooled oil on medium heat and add the asafoetida powder and cumin seeds. Sauté them, till the cumin seeds crackle and releases their aroma and the asafoetida powder melts into the oil.

5 Add the masala paste and continue to sauté or bhuno it, till the water is reduced by half and the oil begins to surface.

6 Once the spices are properly cooked and their raw aroma disappears, add the cubed potatoes. Turn up the heat and toss them in the spices and

mustard oil, till they are well coated. The potatoes will begin to take on a rich mustardy golden yellow colour, which is fantastic.

7 Season well with salt and mix again. Add a few drops of water, turn the heat to a simmer, cover the pan and cook the potatoes, till they are perfectly cooked, but ensure that they do not disintegrate.

8 Uncover the pan, stir everything well, check for salt and add some if required.

9 Now quickly heat 1 tbsp of mustard oil, in a tempering spoon or pan, while retaining its thickness and yellow colour. Add the red chillies and coriander leaves and fry them, till crisp and wonderfully aromatic.

10 Spoon the tempering over the potatoes and stir it in gently. Squeeze in the lime juice to give it zest.

11 Check for a balance of flavours: the potatoes should be really tender and packed with the tang of the spices and mustard oil. The cumin should complement the potatoes perfectly with the tempering lending a great contrast of flavours.

12 Serve it as a side dish in any main meal. It is great on its own with parantha, too.

Aloo Posto
(Potatoes with Poppy Seeds)
6 SERVINGS

A simple and delicious potato recipe from Bengal with poppy seed paste. Deep-frying the potatoes makes the dish really unique. The cumin in the recipe is optional but is recommended as cumin always goes well with potatoes.

Ingredients

THE POPPY SEED PASTE

3 tbsp poppy seeds

3 hot green chillies

½ tsp cumin seeds

¼ tsp salt

THE ALOO POSTO

6–8 medium-sized potatoes

2 cups mustard oil

3 dried red chillies

½ tsp turmeric powder

½ tsp salt

Juice of ½ a lime

2–3 tsp chopped fresh coriander leaves

Method

1 First, to make the poppy seed paste, dry-roast the seeds with the green chillies and cumin seeds on medium heat, till the poppy seeds turn chestnut brown and have a nutty aroma. Once the ingredients release their oils and are glossy, turn off the heat and transfer to a spice grinder with a little water.

2 Add some salt and grind to make a fine paste. Taste it for heat as it should be quite hot and nutty. Set aside.

3 Peel the potatoes and cut them into medium-sized cubes.

4 Place the mustard oil in a deep frying pan on high heat till it smokes, to burn off its bitterness. Carefully add the potatoes and shallow-fry them in the hot oil, till they are golden brown and crisp on all sides. Remove them with a slotted spoon and set aside.

THE ALOO POSTO

5 Now, to make the aloo posto, drain off most of the oil used to fry the potatoes and reserve about 2 tbsp in the pan.

6 Reheat the pan, add the red chillies. Sauté on low to medium heat, till they are crisp and fragrant. Add the poppy seed paste and sauté on medium heat for 4–5 minutes.

7 Mix in the turmeric powder and bhuno the paste and spices with a little water, till the oil begins to surface.

8 Once the masala base is a rich yellowy brown, add the fried potatoes and stir together to coat them with the poppy seed paste and spices. Season well with salt, add a little water, stir and cover the pan. Cook on low to medium heat, till the potatoes are perfectly cooked and soft.

9 Uncover the pan and reduce for a few minutes to intensify the flavours and crisp up the potatoes nicely. Stir well to mix the masala and coat the potatoes well.

10 Squeeze in the lime juice and sprinkle the coriander leaves. The potatoes should be crisp, with a nutty poppy and chilli-based masala.

11 Serve hot with a dal and meat dish, and rice or roti.

Amritsari Paneer Bhurji
(Amritsari Indian Cottage Cheese)

3–4 SERVINGS

The most authentic version of paneer bhurji is from Amritsar in Punjab, where it is one of the more popular street foods. Made with soft paneer, it is not only absolutely delicious, it is very simple to make. It is also a great sandwich or toasty filling and is a favourite as school tiffin in several families.

Ingredients

400 gms fresh paneer	¼ tsp sugar
1 tsp refined oil	2 green chillies, chopped
1 tbsp butter	½ tsp dried mango powder
1 tsp cumin seeds	**TO COMPLETE THE DISH**
¼" cassia stick	Juice of ½ a lime
1 medium-sized onion, chopped fine	3 tsp chopped fresh coriander leaves
½" ginger, chopped fine	1 tbsp butter
½ tsp turmeric powder	
1 tsp coriander powder	
½–¾ tsp salt	
1 large ripe tomato, chopped fine	

Method

1 Crumble the paneer and set aside.

2 Heat a medium-sized frying pan and add the oil. Swirl the pan to coat it well. Once the oil is hot, add the butter and let it melt and foam. Now add the cumin seeds and cassia stick and sauté them on medium heat, till crackled and aromatic.

3 Add the onion and sauté on medium heat, till it turns light golden. Throw in the chopped ginger and sauté, till soft.

4 Sprinkle in the spice powders and sauté on high heat, till nicely toasted.

5 Add the salt and bhuno the masala with a little water, deglazing and combining, till the aromatic spice base is fully cooked and the oil begins to rise to the surface.

6 Add the tomato and sauté, till it is soft and fully cooked. Mix in the sugar to balance the acidity of the tomatoes.

7 When the masala is homogenous and the oil has surfaced, add the green chillies, mango powder and crumbled paneer. Mix the paneer with the masala, till it's fully coated with the spices.

8 Stir everything together to combine, cover the pan and simmer the bhurji for about 10 minutes to cook it through to perfection.

9 Uncover the pan and break up the paneer to resemble scrambled eggs.

10 Once the paneer is cooked and the oil rises to the surface, turn off the heat.

TO COMPLETE THE DISH

11 Squeeze in the lime juice and sprinkle the coriander leaves. Add a little more butter and stir through.

12 Check for a balance of flavours: the paneer should be soft and creamy in texture and full of the simple, rustic spices and aromatics. The butter should come through gently and the coriander leaves and lime should lift the flavours of this delicate and delicious paneer bhurji perfectly.

13 Serve with hot buttered bread rolls, parantha, roti, or pao bread, or use it as a sandwich spread.

Beetroot Pachadi
(Beetroot Relish)
6 SERVINGS

A simple and colourful side dish, this pachadi is full of the goodness of fresh beetroots. It requires a minimal amount of cooking, and is really exotic in its flavour. The beetroot can be substituted by vegetables with a similar firm texture, such as carrots, daikon radish, turnips, other root vegetables and even green beans. The results are always superb.

Ingredients

5–6 medium-sized beet-roots (peeled and grated)

THE PACHADI BASE

3 tsp coconut oil

1 tsp mustard seeds

A small handful of curry leaves

7–8 shallots, julienned

¼" ginger, sliced

2 green chillies, split

½ cup of grated fresh coconut

¼ tsp cumin powder

½ tsp coriander powder

2 tbsp thick tamarind extract (see page 10)

½ tsp grated jaggery to balance

½ tsp salt

4 tbsp whisked curd

Method

1 Peel the beetroots, grate them and set aside.

THE PACHADI

2 Heat the coconut oil in a medium-sized kadhai. Turn the heat to medium and add the mustard seeds and curry leaves. Fry, till they crackle and smell nutty and aromatic.

3 Add the shallots and ginger and sauté, till softened but not coloured. Then add the green chillies and sauté for a couple of minutes longer.

4 Add some of the grated coconut, reserving 1–2 tbsp for the garnish. Fry for a few minutes, till the coconut is fragrant and glossy with its natural oils.

5 Sprinkle in the spice powders, tamarind extract and jaggery. Add a little water to deglaze the pan and sauté the base for a few minutes to combine everything.

6 Add the grated beetroot and season well with salt. Stir a few times to coat the beetroot in the delicate, simple base.

7 Mix in a little water, cover the kadhai and let the beetroot steam for 8–10 minutes or till it's perfectly cooked but still has some bite to it. Turn off the heat and let it cool.

8 Add the curd and stir it in gently to combine well and coat the beetroot perfectly, giving it a delicate pinkish colour and a slightly sour kick.

9 Scatter some of the reserved freshly grated coconut on top and serve warm or cold.

Moru Sambhar
(Okra and Aubergine in a Curd-Based Curry)

....

There are literally hundreds of different sambhar recipes in South India. This buttermilk version is to my mind rather unusual and delicate, and tastes fantastic with steamed rice and a pickle.

Method

THE VEGETABLES

1 First par-cook the vegetables. Heat a medium-sized pan and add 3 tsp of coconut oil. When the oil is hot, add the turmeric powder and chilli powder and sauté for a minute. Add the okra and fry them in the spices, till they are well coated.

2 Pour in the tamarind extract and sauté for a couple of minutes on medium heat. Then pour in ½ cup of water and stir everything together to combine well. Cover the pan and simmer, till the okra begins to soften and absorb the sour tamarind and spices.

3 Add the aubergines and toss them in the rich juices in the pan, till they are well coated.

4 Sprinkle in the salt, cover the pan and simmer, till the okra are tender and the aubergines are about half cooked. Turn off the heat and set aside, uncovered, to prevent the vegetables from overcooking in the residual heat of the pan.

THE SAMBHAR MASALA

5 To make the sambhar masala, dry-roast all the ingredients in a hot frying pan, while reserving a little grated coconut for the tempering. Roast them, till they release their natural oils and are aromatic. Transfer to a heavy mortar or grinder, add a little water and grind to make a fine paste. The masala

should be really nutty and sweet with the coconut, and robust with all the strong spices. The fenugreek seeds give it their trademark, mild bitterness.

THE SAMBHAR

6 Put a deep pan on medium heat. Add 3 tsp of coconut oil and swirl the pan to coat it well. Once the oil is hot, add the sambhar masala paste and sauté it on medium to high heat. Add a little water and bhuno, till it is a deep, rich brown.

7 Mix in the tamarind extract and jaggery and continue to bhuno the masala, till the oil rises to the surface. Turn the heat down to low and slowly add the diluted curd, a little at a time, stirring continuously, to combine it well with the masala.

8 Add the salt and simmer the sambhar for 10–15 minutes or till the curry is a light, yellow-brown and the oil has begun to surface again.

9 Now, add the par-cooked vegetables with the tamarind-flavoured juices and simmer, till they are almost cooked through. Stir everything together to mix well.

10 Bring the sambhar up to a gentle boil to amalgamate the flavours, then turn the heat to the barest possible simmer and cook uncovered to reduce it a little and concentrate the gravy.

The Chakh le India Cookbook

Ingredients

THE VEGETABLES

500 gms okra, chopped into ½" pieces

6 small, round aubergines, halved with stems intact

3 tsp coconut oil

½ tsp turmeric powder

½ tsp mild red chilli powder

2 tbsp thick tamarind extract (see page 10)

½ tsp salt

THE SAMBHAR MASALA

2 tbsp urad dal or husked, split black gram

2 tbsp tuvar/arhar dal or pigeon peas

1 tsp cumin seeds

½ tsp fenugreek seeds

1 tsp coriander seeds

½ tsp whole black peppercorns

6 garlic cloves

½" ginger

1 cup grated fresh coconut

½ tsp turmeric powder

1 tsp mild red chilli powder

½ tsp salt to help grind

THE SAMBHAR BASE

3 tsp coconut oil

2 tbsp tamarind extract (see page 10)

½–¾ tsp grated jaggery, to balance

1½ cups curd whisked with 1½ cups water

¾ tsp salt

THE TEMPERING

3 tsp coconut oil

4–5 mild dried red chillies

½ tsp mustard seeds

A small handful of curry leaves

1 tbsp grated fresh coconut

¼ tsp sea salt

---

11 Once the oil rises to the surface and the sambhar is perfectly cooked, fry the tempering ingredients in 3 tsp of hot coconut oil, till they crackle and are aromatic. Add them to the simmering sambhar, giving it a contrast of colours and a delicate sheen from the oil on the surface. Turn off the heat.

12 Check for a balance of flavours: the sambhar should be delicately sour with the curd and tamarind, and a complex and slightly bitter note of the masala coming through on the finish. The vegetables should be perfectly tender and full of the flavours of the sambhar gravy. The tempering should provide a little contrast of taste and texture to the sambhar.

13 Serve with steamed rice and enjoy.

Bendakkai Gojju
(Okra with Tamarind)

The humble lady fingers or okra are transformed into a deliciously sweet-sour, coconut-flavoured delight in this typically South Indian vegetable dish. This recipe is undoubtedly one of the best techniques to turn everyday vegetables into a real treat.

Ingredients

500 gms okra (topped and left whole, washed)	A handful of fresh coriander leaves and stems
3–4 tsp + 2 tsp refined oil	Salt
½–¾ tsp salt	½ tsp turmeric powder
THE MASALA PASTE	3 tbsp of thick tamarind extract (see page 10)
1 tsp fenugreek seeds	¼ tsp jaggery
1 tsp sesame seeds	**THE TEMPERING**
1 tsp cumin seeds	½ tbsp oil
¼ tsp whole black peppercorns	4–5 dried red chillies
¾ cup grated fresh coconut	½ tsp mustard seeds
1 tsp rice grains	¼ tsp fenugreek seeds
½ tsp mustard seeds	
4 medium-hot green chillies	

Method

1 Wash the okra and dry immediately on kitchen towels. Top them and keep whole.

2 Heat a medium-sized frying pan and add 3–4 tsp of oil. Swirl the pan to coat it well. Once it's hot, add the okra. Fry on medium heat, till they begin to take on a lovely golden brown colour. Add some salt to season and fry for a few minutes longer.

3 Once the okra is crisp, brown and well coated in the oil, turn off the heat and remove the okra to another bowl. Set aside.

MASALA PASTE

4 To make the masala paste, dry-roast all the ingredients, except the tamarind extract and jaggery, in a hot frying pan, till they release their aromas and natural oils. Transfer the ingredients to a spice grinder, add the jaggery and tamarind extract with a little water and grind to make a really fine paste.

THE CURRY

5 To create the base for the curry, heat 2 tsp of oil in a pan. Add the spice paste and sauté it on medium heat. Sprinkle in a few drops of water to incorporate everything and fry the spices, till the oil begins to surface and the paste is a deep rich brown.

6 Add the fried okra and stir to coat them with the spicy, tangy masala paste. Fry the okra in the paste for a few minutes, till they absorb the flavours well. Add a couple of cups of water and stir to mix well.

7 Bring to a boil and turn the heat down to a simmer. Cook the okra, till they are perfectly tender but still holding their shape. They should absorb all the spices and tamarind extract and the gravy should be semi-thick. The coconut and rice grains serve as thickening agents for the curry.

THE TEMPERING

8 Next, prepare the tempering by frying the temper ingredients in hot oil, till they crackle to release their aromas. Spoon the tempering into the simmering okra curry and stir through to combine well.

9 Bring the curry to a boil to amalgamate the flavours.

10 Check for a balance of flavours: the curry should be semi-thick and concentrated with the spices and tamarind, and perfectly balanced with the jaggery.

11 Serve the bendakkai gojju with steamed rice.

Beetroot Pachadi
Pg 111

Aloo Posto
Pg 109

Amritsari Paneer Burji
Pg 110

Carrot Gojju
Pg 119

Coorgi Baby Jackfruit Curry

4–6 SERVINGS

Jackfruit grows wild all over Coorg. It is cooked in several different ways and develops the texture of meat when cooked. Baby jackfruit is really tender and doesn't need long cooking. In this recipe, the robust spices and sweet nuttiness of the coconut brings out its delicate flavour perfectly.

Ingredients

1 small baby jackfruit

THE MASALA PASTE

1 heaped tsp coriander seeds

2 tsp whole black peppercorns

½" cassia stick

1 cup grated fresh coconut

6–8 garlic cloves

½" fresh ginger

½ tsp turmeric powder

½ tsp salt

THE CURRY BASE

3–4 tsp refined oil

3 whole dried red chillies

A few curry leaves

½ tsp mustard seeds

2 medium-sized onions, julienned

½ tsp salt

Juice of 1 lime

Method

1 Peel the jackfruit and chop it into segments.

2 Put a little water in a medium-sized pan and bring to a boil. Put the jackfruit into a sieve and place it on the pan, making sure that the water does not touch the jackfruit. Cover with a plate, turn the heat down to low and steam the jackfruit, till tender.

3 Remove the jackfruit to a chopping board and let it cool. Trim off the tough rind and chop the flesh into small pieces. Set aside.

THE MASALA PASTE

4 To make the masala paste, dry-roast all the masala paste ingredients together in a small frying pan, till they release their oils and are aromatic. Grind in a heavy mortar or grinder, till almost fine in consistency. Set aside.

THE CURRY

5 To make the curry, heat a deep-sided pan and add the oil. Swirl the pan to coat its base. Add the red chillies, curry leaves and mustard seeds and let them crackle on medium heat, till fragrant. Add the onions and sauté, till slightly coloured and soft.

6 Now add the ground masala paste and bhuno, using a little water to combine well and cook the spices fully. When the oil rises to the surface, it is a sure sign that the spices are cooked and the base of the curry is ready.

7 Add the steamed baby jackfruit and fry it in the base to coat well.

8 Sprinkle in the salt and mix well. Pour in 1 cup of water and deglaze the pan. Cover and cook, till the jackfruit is tender and has absorbed all the wonderful flavours of the spices and coconut. The gravy should be thick.

9 Check for seasovvning and squeeze in some lime juice if required.

10 Serve hot with ghee rice.

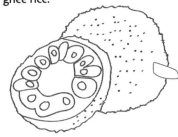

Chana Madra
(Sweet and Sour Slow-Cooked Chickpeas)

8 SERVINGS

A staple in the cold climate of Himachal Pradesh, this is part of a traditional dham in the region. It's a delicate sweet and sour dish made with creamy chickpeas and plump raisins. The aromatic garam masala gives it an exotic twist. It can be made with red kidney beans as well.

Ingredients

THE CHICKPEAS

2 cups chickpeas

2 tbsp ghee

½ tsp salt

3 tbsp green seedless raisins

1 litre buttermilk or chaas

THE GARAM MASALA

6–7 cloves

¼ tsp whole black peppercorns

½ tsp cumin seeds

1 tsp coriander seeds

½" cassia stick

2 brown cardamoms

¼" dried ginger

Method

THE CHICKPEAS

1 Wash the chickpeas and soak them in water overnight. Drain and rinse thoroughly to remove any toxins that may have formed.

2 Parboil the chickpeas in boiling water, till they are semi-soft. Drain and set aside.

THE GARAM MASALA

3 To make the garam masala, dry-roast the spices in a hot pan, till fragrant. Transfer to a mortar or grinder and grind it to a fine consistency.

TO COOK THE MADRA

4 Heat a heavy, deep pan and add the ghee. When it melts, swirl the pan to coat its base. Add the parboiled chickpeas and season well. Fry the chickpeas in the ghee on medium heat, till they are glossy and begin to take on a nutty, light brown colour.

5 Add the garam masala and fry the chickpeas with the spices, till the raw aroma of the masala disappears.

6 Add the raisins and continue frying on medium heat, till they are soft and plump. The raisins lend a delicate sweetness to this recipe.

7 Pour in the buttermilk and stir well to combine all the ingredients.

8 Cover the pan with a tight-fitting lid, turn the heat down to the barest possible simmer and cook the chickpeas slowly for 2–3 hours or till they start to break down slightly, but retain some of their shape.

9 As the chickpeas cook, the starch will break down to thicken the buttermilk-based gravy. It should have the consistency of a liquid rajmah (red kidney beans cooked with spices, aromatics and tomatoes).

10 Check for a balance of flavours and season if necessary: the madra should be delicately sweet from the raisins and sour from the buttermilk. The chickpeas should be creamy and hold their shape partially, but have a soft, mushy texture.

11 Serve hot with chapati or steamed rice.

Note: Slow-cooking such a bean dish gently coaxes out the starch, making it wonderfully creamy, thick and wholesome.

Carrot Gojju
(Carrot with Mustard and Curry Leaves)

4 SERVINGS

A delicious South Indian way of turning simple carrots into a tangy, spicy, coconut delight. The southern spice combination can be used for a variety of other vegetables. For a simpler and fresher variation, omit the masala paste and cook the carrots with the aromatics and tamarind. Lovely!

Ingredients

5 carrots

THE MASALA PASTE

1 tbsp coconut oil

½" ginger

4 hot green chillies

1 tsp cumin seeds

1 tsp coriander seeds

½ tsp black sesame seeds

1 tsp husked, split Bengal gram or chana dal

A small handful of fresh coriander leaves and stems

½ cup grated fresh coconut

½ tsp salt

THE GOJJU BASE

2 tsp coconut oil

½ tsp mustard seeds

A handful of curry leaves

2 tsp thick tamarind extract (see page 10)

¼ tsp grated jaggery

¼ tsp salt

THE GARNISH

Juice of ½–¾ of a lime

2–3 tsp chopped fresh coriander leaves

Method

1. Peel the carrots and slice them into fine matchstick-sized juliennes or grate them coarsely.

THE MASALA PASTE

2. To make the masala paste, heat the coconut oil in a kadhai or wok. Add the ginger and green chillies and sauté on medium heat, till fragrant and aromatic.

3. Add the whole spices, gram, coriander leaves and stems, coconut and salt and fry them all together, till they begin to colour slightly and are intensely aromatic.

4. Transfer to a heavy mortar or grinder. Add a little water and grind, till it has a semi-fine consistency. Set aside.

THE GOJJU

5. Now for the base, heat 2 tsp of coconut oil in the same kadhai used for the masala paste. When it is hot, add the mustard seeds and curry leaves and fry, till they crackle and release their aromas.

6. Stir in the fresh green masala paste and bhuno it with a little water, till it turns a rich green colour and the oil begins to rise to the surface.

7. Pour in the tamarind extract and continue to sauté for a few minutes longer, to combine well.

8. Add the jaggery, salt and carrots and stir everything well to combine and coat the carrots in the thick, spicy-sour coconut masala.

9. Pour in a little water and deglaze the kadhai, lifting up the rich pan deposits on the base. Mix everything together well, cover and steam the carrots for 3–4 minutes to cook through.

10. Uncover the pan and turn up the heat to reduce and concentrate the gojju.

11. Turn off the heat, squeeze in the lime juice and sprinkle the coriander leaves.

12. Check for a balance of flavours: the carrots should be perfectly cooked but still retain a delicate crunch. The fresh spicy green masala should taste of coconut and be sour and hot with the green chillies. It should coat the carrots perfectly. The lime and coriander leaves should help lift the flavours.

13. Serve the gojju as a perfect side dish or eat it on its own.

Snack
RECIPES

Chicken 65
Pg 130

Hara Bhara Kabab

(Fresh Herb Kabab)

4–5 SERVINGS

Although kababs are generally associated with meat, here is a real classic party favourite. These lovely fresh veggie kababs invite variation and imagination. The potatoes and corn starch act as binding agents and give the kababs their body. Keep the mixture a little coarse for some added texture and bite. Healthy and tasty!

Ingredients

- 3 large potatoes
- A handful of shelled fresh green peas
- 2 cups spinach
- ½ tsp cumin powder
- 1 tsp coriander powder
- ½ tsp turmeric powder
- ½ tsp dried mango powder
- ¾ tsp salt
- ¼" ginger
- 4–5 garlic cloves
- ¼ cup chopped fresh coriander leaves
- 2 hot green chillies
- Juice of ½ a lime
- 1 tsp refined oil plus extra for shallow-frying
- 1 tbsp cornflour
- 1 tbsp butter

Method

1 Scrub the potatoes, boil them, peel and set aside.

2 Add the green peas to a pan of boiling water and cook for 3–5 minutes, till par-cooked. Add the spinach to the pan and cook till they just wilt.

3 Drain and refresh the green peas and spinach under cold running water. Drain and squeeze out most of the water. Chop them up coarsely and set aside.

4 Put 2 boiled potatoes with the spinach and green peas into a blender. Add the spice powders, mango powder, salt, ginger, garlic, coriander leaves, green chillies, lime juice, and 1 tsp of oil. Blend the ingredients, till they form a thick, bright green mixture that is semi-fine in consistency.

5 Transfer the mixture to a bowl. Mash the remaining boiled potato and add it to the mix along with the cornflour to give it some body and help bind the kabab mix. The mixture will now become fairly tight and sticky which is perfect.

6 To make the kababs, wet your palms to avoid the mixture from sticking, and shape the mixture into equal-sized, flat, round disks about ½" in thickness. Place them on a floured plate, cover and put them into the refrigerator to set for about 30 minutes.

7 Once the kababs are chilled and firm, remove them from the refrigerator and bring to room temperature.

8 Heat the oil for shallow-frying in a non-stick frying pan with the butter. Add 3–4 kababs at a time, and fry them gently on medium heat, till crisp and golden brown on both sides. Remove, drain on kitchen paper and put them into a low oven to keep warm.

9 Arrange the kababs on a white platter and serve with a tangy, spicy tamarind chutney.

Snack Recipes

Paneer Tikka
(Indian Cottage Cheese Kabab)
6 SERVINGS

....

Once again, a snack which cuts across geographies and emerges as one of the more favoured in India. Delicious, fresh chunks of Indian cottage cheese or paneer, marinated in plenty of spices and aromatics, it is best when cooked over a hot charcoal fire. However this snack tastes equally delectable when done in the oven and roasted as given.

Method

1 Cut the paneer into 1" cubes, the capsicum into 1" square pieces and the onions into 1" wedges or petals. Cut the tomatoes in half, along the equator and squeeze out the seeds. Slice the tomato flesh into 1" petals. Set aside.

THE GARAM MASALA

2 To make the garam masala, dry-roast the whole spices in a small, hot frying pan, till they are aromatic. Transfer them to a mortar or grinder and grind to make a fine powder. Set aside.

THE MARINADE

3 To make the marinade, put the ginger-garlic paste, spice powders, salt, fresh chopped herbs, green chillies, lime juice, oil, curd and 2 tsp of the freshly ground garam masala in a bowl. Mix really well with a fork, till the marinade is a rich yellow-red colour.

4 Taste the marinade to check for a balance of spices and salt. Add a little more garam masala if required.

5 Put the paneer and vegetables into a roasting pan and pour on the marinade.

6 Mix it in gently to coat the paneer and vegetables really well. Cover the pan and put it into the refrigerator for about an hour. The curd will form a thick coating along with the complex flavours of the spices and aromatics and also tenderize the paneer.

7 The paneer can be marinated for more than an hour. For instance, if they are to be served in the evening, they can be marinated in the morning for excellent results.

TO COOK THE TIKKA

8 Remove the paneer and vegetables from the refrigerator and bring to room temperature.

9 Soak the satay bamboo sticks in water for about 20 minutes or so, to prevent them from burning in the oven.

10 To skewer, start with a chunk of paneer, followed by onion and capsicum, then the paneer and tomato. Or arrange them in any other order, as long as some vegetables are skewered between two pieces of paneer. Place the skewers in the same roasting pan.

124

Ingredients

1 kg fresh paneer	1 brown cardamom	½ tsp chaat masala
3 green capsicums	4 green cardamoms	1–1½ tsp salt
2 onions	¼ tsp black cumin seeds	A handful of fresh coriander leaves, chopped fine
3 tomatoes	¼ pod of star anise	
6–8 satay bamboo sticks	½ tsp whole black peppercorns	A handful of fresh mint leaves, chopped fine
Refined oil as required	**THE MARINADE**	
2 limes, cut into wedges	3 tsp ginger-garlic paste	2 green chillies, chopped fine
THE GARAM MASALA	¾ tsp turmeric powder	Juice of ½ a lime
1 tsp cumin seeds	1 tsp medium-hot red chilli powder	2 tsp refined oil
1 tsp coriander seeds	½ tsp Kashmiri red chilli powder	2 cups whisked curd
4–5 cloves	½ tsp dried mango powder	

11 Coat the skewer with excess marinade, and drizzle with a little oil to keep them moist and to crisp them up nicely.

12 Preheat an oven to 180°C.

13 Roast the tikka in the oven, till the thick marinade is a rich, deep, yellow-red in colour, the paneer and vegetables begin to char slightly and the raw aroma of spices disappears. This should take 20–25 minutes in a hot oven.

14 Alternatively, roast them on a hot, oiled, non-stick tava.

15 Once the tikkas are cooked through and sizzling, place the skewers on a platter. Squeeze some fresh lime juice on top and serve.

16 Check for a balance of flavours: the tikka should be delicate, with a complexity of flavours from the marinade. The paneer should melt in the mouth and the vegetables should be charred and slightly crunchy.

Semolina-Coated Prawn Fry

4 SERVINGS

These crisp, golden-fried prawns are very easy to prepare and make the perfect appetizer or snack for a cocktail or dinner party. As an alternative, they can be baked in an oven for a lighter version.

Ingredients

6–8 large tiger prawns

THE MARINADE

3 tsp ginger-garlic paste

½ tsp turmeric powder

½ tsp medium-hot red chilli powder

1 tsp coriander powder

1 tsp refined oil

¾ tsp salt

TO COAT AND FRY

Refined oil to deep-fry

250 gms toasted coarse semolina or rava

Method

The Chakh le India Cookbook

1 The first thing to do is to prepare the prawns. Peel them and take off the heads, leaving the tails intact. Make a shallow cut down the spine of the prawns and remove the veins. Wash the prawns under cold running water and drain thoroughly.

2 Using the same knife, gently slice down the back three-quarters of the way down, to open up the prawn like a butterfly. This increases their surface area a little more and helps the marinade to penetrate the flesh. Put the prawns in a bowl, cover and put them in the refrigerator.

THE MARINADE

3 To make the marinade, put all the ingredients into a small bowl and mix them well to get a smooth, yellow-red paste of fine consistency.

4 Remove the prawns from the refrigerator and uncover. Add the marinade and gently massage it into the prawns. Cover again and put them into the refrigerator to marinate for about 15 minutes.

TO COAT AND FRY THE PRAWNS

5 To crumb the prawns, spread some of the semolina on a plate and add a prawn to it. Press the prawn into the semolina gently, coating it in a thick layer on all sides, making sure that it is fully encased in the semolina. The thick spice paste will add as an adhesive for the semolina and help create a uniform coating while flavouring it perfectly from within.

6 Repeat with all the prawns, and then put the semolina-coated prawns into the refrigerator for 5–10 minutes, not only to set the coating but also to get a crisper, crunchier texture.

7 Heat the oil in a deep pan, till it reaches the right temperature for deep frying. Test by frying a cube of bread in the oil. If it fries evenly to a deep golden brown in 2–3 minutes, the oil is ready for frying.

8 Remove the prawns from the refrigerator and gently add two at a time to the hot oil. Deep-fry the prawns, till they are light golden and the semolina coating is perfectly crisp.

9 Once all the prawns are perfectly golden fried, place them on a white platter and serve straight away with a tangy tamarind chutney.

Reshmi Murgh Tikka
(Silky Chicken Kabab)

3–4 SERVINGS

These silky smooth chicken tikkas are a real classic and loved all over India, and overseas too. Try them once and you're sure to be making them again and again!

Ingredients

500 gms boneless chicken	4 tbsp whisked curd
THE GARAM MASALA	½–¾ tsp salt
1 tsp cumin seeds	1 tsp refined oil
1 tsp coriander seeds	Juice of ½ a lime
½ tsp whole black peppercorns	1 tbsp of the fresh garam masala
½" cassia stick	**TO COOK AND SERVE THE KABABS**
4–5 cloves	
4–5 green cardamoms	1–2 tsp butter
THE MARINADE	1–2 tsp chopped fresh coriander leaves
3–4 tsp ginger-garlic paste	Juice of 1 lime
½ tsp turmeric powder	
3–4 tbsp heavy cream	

Method

1. Cut the chicken into kabab-sized chunks. Wash the chicken pieces well and drain thoroughly. Put them into a bowl, cover and set aside.

THE GARAM MASALA

2. To make the garam masala, dry-roast all the whole spices in a small frying pan, till they release their oils and are intensely fragrant. Transfer them to a heavy mortar or grinder and grind them to a fine powder. Reserve.

THE MARINADE

3. To marinate the chicken, put all the marinade ingredients into a large bowl and mix well.

4. Add the chicken and massage the marinade into it, making sure the pieces are evenly coated. Cover the bowl and put it in the refrigerator to marinate for 2–4 hours.

TO COOK AND SERVE THE TIKKA

5. Once the chicken has been marinated, remove it from the refrigerator and bring to room temperature.

6. Preheat an oven to 180ºC.

7. Soak 3–4 metal or wooden skewers in water for 15 minutes.

8. Skewer the chicken pieces through the centre, keeping them close to each other. Place them in a roasting tray and put into the hot oven.

9. Roast the kababs for 15–20 minutes, turning them around halfway through the process and basting them with a little butter to enhance the taste and colour.

10. When the kababs are light golden brown and the marinade has formed a thick coating on the outside, test the chicken by piercing it with a knife. If the juices run clear, the chicken is cooked.

11. Remove the kababs from the oven and leave them to rest for a few minutes.

12. Carefully push them off the hot skewers on to a serving platter.

13. Squeeze some lime juice over them to give them a fresh citrus kick. Sprinkle with coriander leaves and serve the kababs immediately.

Kathi Kabab

(Spicy Mutton Wraps)

4 SERVINGS

....

An all-time favourite with kids and grown-ups alike, these delicious little mutton rolls make the perfect "anytime" meal or snack. An easy-to-make and complete meal in itself, the toppings could be experimented with or just the way this recipe recommends.

Method

1 Cut the meat into kabab-sized chunks, trim and wash them. Drain thoroughly.

THE MARINADE

2 Combine all the marinade ingredients in a large bowl. Mix well with your hands to make a fine, reddish, yellow paste. Add the meat and massage the marinade into it thoroughly, till the chunks are evenly coated.

3 Cover the marinated meat and put it into the refrigerator for 2–4 hours.

TO COOK THE MEAT

4 Before pan-frying the kababs, remove the meat from the refrigerator and bring it to room temperature. Season the meat liberally with salt.

5 Heat a heavy frying pan and add a little oil. Swirl the pan to coat it well. When the oil is hot, add 6–7 chunks of meat to the pan and sear them evenly on all sides, till they are richly browned, with a caramelized crust on the outside. Remove the browned chunks and put them on a plate.

6 Sear the remaining chunks in the same way, adding more oil and butter to the pan as required.

7 Once all the chunks have been browned, return them to the pan. Add a little butter for colour and taste and fry well.

8 Sprinkle in a little water and deglaze the pan well, scraping up the rich, caramelized pan deposits. Stir the meat and deglaze the pan with water a few times to combine well. Then turn the heat down, cover the pan and cook on medium heat for 15 minutes or till the meat is tender and cooked through.

9 Uncover the pan and turn the heat up to reduce the rich, brown pan juices, till the masala is thick and coats the chunks richly, and the oil has risen to the surface.

10 When most of the moisture has dried up, mix the meat well and turn off the heat. Add a little more butter if required and squeeze in lime juice to lift the meaty flavours.

Ingredients

500 gms boneless leg
  of lamb or mutton

1 tsp salt

2 tsp refined oil

1½ tsp butter

Juice of 1 lime

THE MARINADE

3 tsp ginger-garlic paste

½ tsp turmeric powder

1 tsp medium-hot red chilli powder

1 tsp coriander powder

½ tsp cumin powder

Juice of 1 lime

2 green chillies, chopped fine

2 tsp refined oil

THE ROLL

4 home-made paranthas

Refined oil to warm the paranthas

2 onions, cut into fine juliennes

6–8 fresh coriander leaves

4 tsp chopped fresh mint leaves

3 green chillies, seeded
  and chopped fine

Juice of 1 lime

A pinch of chaat masala powder

11 Leave the meat to rest in a warm place to relax and reabsorb its juices.

TO ASSEMBLE THE ROLLS

12 In the meanwhile, heat a tava or frying pan and add a little oil. Once the oil is hot, put a parantha on it and fry it in the oil, till it is hot and crisp on both sides. Remove and keep warm. Repeat with the remaining paranthas, adding more oil to the tava, as required.

13 To assemble the kathi rolls, lay the fried parantha on a chopping board. Put a good quantity of the meat chunks along one side of the parantha. Scatter some onions, coriander leaves, mint leaves and a pinch of chaat masala. Squeeze a little lime juice on top.

14 Roll the parantha to make a tightly-filled kathi roll and wrap it in a little aluminium foil or butter paper to secure the roll and make it easy to hold and eat.

15 Roll all the kathis in the same way and serve them with a mint and green chilli chutney.

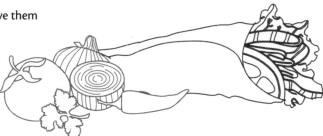

Chicken 65

4–5 SERVINGS

....

I wonder if this is the Indian version of batter-fried chicken that is now so popular across all age groups! Well it definitely could be, as it's delicious, with a similar deep red, crispy batter and succulent, flavoursome marinated pieces of chicken.

Method

1 Cut the chicken breasts into long, thin strips and put them into a bowl.

THE MARINADE

2 Combine the marinade ingredients in a small bowl and mix, till well blended. Add it to the chicken and rub it in thoroughly, till the strips are generously coated in the aromatic masala paste. Cover and put into the refrigerator for an hour.

THE BATTER

3 Meanwhile, prepare the batter for coating the chicken. Put the cornflour and refined flour in a bowl with the salt and spice powders. Mix with a fork, till the flour is a deep red colour.

4 Now add the chilled club soda and beat the mixture with a fork or whisk a few times to get a batter of coating consistency. Ensure that the batter isn't overworked, as that would knock out the gas bubbles of the soda, and the batter would lose its lightness.

5 Put the batter into the refrigerator to rest for about 30 minutes. This is mandatory as it allows the gluten in the batter to form stronger strands with the liquid, thus helping it to adhere to the food considerably better.

TO FRY THE CHICKEN

6 Once the chicken is marinated and the batter rested, remove both from the refrigerator and bring them to room temperature. Loosen the batter with a little more club soda and gently stir it once or twice.

7 Heat the oil for deep-frying in a wok, till it reaches the perfect deep-frying temperature. To test the temperature, dip a strip of chicken in the batter, shake off the excess batter and slide it into the hot oil. Deep-fry the piece on high heat to check the temperature of the oil. The piece should deep-fry evenly within 4–5 minutes. The batter should turn deep reddish brown and the chicken should be perfectly moist as well as crisp.

8 Once a piece passes this test, dip 5–6 chicken strips into the batter and shaking off the excess to get the lightest and thinnest possible coating.

Ingredients

4 boneless chicken breasts without skin

Refined oil to deep-fry the chicken

THE MARINADE

2 tbsp ginger-garlic paste

¾ tsp salt

1 tsp red chilli powder

½ tsp turmeric powder

1 tsp coriander powder

1 tsp refined oil

THE BATTER

5–6 tbsp cornflour

1 tbsp refined flour

½ tsp salt

1 tsp hot red chilli powder

½ tsp red Kashmiri chilli powder

¼ tsp turmeric powder

½ tsp cumin powder

Chilled club soda

THE TEMPERING

6 dried red chillies

1 tsp mustard seeds

A few curry leaves

Deep-fry the chicken and drain on kitchen paper. Keep warm in a low oven.

9 Once all the chicken is crisp and cooked through, take 1 tbsp of the deep-frying oil and add it to a small frying pan placed on medium heat.

10 When the oil is hot, add the tempering ingredients and fry them, till crackled and crisp. Spoon the hot tempering over the crisp-fried chicken and serve straight away.

11 Enjoy it with onions and any chutney of choice, or even rolled in a roti or parantha with various toppings to make a delicious snack.

12 It can also be served with chilled beer, a tangy tamarind chutney and plenty of lime.

Paneer Pakoda
(Indian Cottage Cheese Fritters)

4–5 SERVINGS

An all-time favourite in india, these delicious Indian cottage cheese or paneer fritters are perfect for a rainy day with a hot cup of tea and lots of friends and family.

Ingredients

250 gms fresh paneer

½ tsp turmeric powder

½ tsp red chilli powder

¼ tsp salt

1 tsp refined oil + extra to deep-fry the pakodas

THE BATTER

1 cup gram flour

½–¾ tsp salt

¼ tsp caraway seeds or ajwain, ground coarsely

2 cups chilled water

Method

1 Cut the paneer into ½" cubes and put them into a bowl.

2 Combine the spice powders, salt and 1 tsp of oil in a small bowl. Mix it with your hands to make a thick paste and then rub the paste into the paneer to coat the pieces evenly. Set aside.

3 To make the batter, put the gram flour into a bowl. Add the salt and spices and mix well.

4 Pour in 1 cup of chilled water and whisk with a fork, till it forms a thick paste. Pour in another cup of chilled water and whisk it well again, breaking up any lumps with the fork, till the batter is really well combined and semi-thin in consistency.

5 Cover the batter and put it into the refrigerator for 15 minutes to help it set.

6 Remove the batter from the refrigerator and stir it a couple of times to mix it well. Add a little water to thin it down, if it appears to have thickened in the refrigerator. The batter should be of a good pouring consistency, but not watery.

7 Heat a deep pan or kadhai and add the oil for deep-frying, till it's really hot and ready for deep-frying. Test the temperature by frying a cube of bread in the oil. If it fries evenly to a deep golden brown in 2–3 minutes, the oil is ready for frying.

8 Dip a few pieces of paneer into the batter. Make sure they are well-coated by the batter and let any of the excess batter drip off.

9 Add the batter-coated paneer pieces to the hot oil and deep-fry them, till they are crisp and golden. Remove them with a slotted spoon and drain the excess oil on kitchen paper.

10 Fry the remaining paneer in the same way.

11 Arrange them on a platter and serve with a tangy or spicy chutney.

Paneer Tikka
Pg 124

Chola Masala
Pg 136

Easy Fish Cutlets
Pg 138

Paneer Pakoda
Pg 132

Mutton Cutlets

4–5 SERVINGS

. . . .

Seldom have I come across anyone who doesn't love a crisp, delicious mutton cutlet. They are immensely popular, not just as a perfect heavy snack, but also as a great main course when served with a fresh salad. Unlike what is presumed, these cutlets are easy and quick to make. The lamb can be substituted with any protein of choice, as also the combination of spices.

Ingredients

- 2 medium-sized potatoes
- 250 gms minced mutton or lamb
- 2 tsp ginger-garlic paste
- ½ tsp turmeric powder
- 1 tsp red chilli powder
- ½ tsp cumin powder
- 1 tsp coriander powder
- 2 green chillies, seeded and chopped fine
- A small handful of fresh coriander leaves, chopped
- Juice of ½ a lime
- 1 tsp refined oil + extra to fry the cutlets
- ¾ tsp salt
- 1 cup fine breadcrumbs
- 2–3 tsp butter

Method

1 Scrub the potatoes and boil them, till tender. Peel and mash them coarsely.

2 Put the mince into a bowl and add the ginger-garlic paste, spice powders, green chillies, coriander leaves, lime juice and 1 tsp of oil.

3 Mix them together thoroughly with your hands and season with salt.

4 Add the mashed potatoes and mix well, to help bind the mixture and give it some body. Knead the mix, till it is firm and holds its shape well.

5 Divide the cutlet mixture into 6 equal balls and shape them into ½" thick, round cutlets, pressing them down to flatten them and then shaping and smoothening out the rough edges gently.

6 Put the cutlets into the refrigerator for about 15 minutes, to set and firm them up.

7 Remove them from the refrigerator and bring to room temperature.

8 Spread the breadcrumbs on a plate. Lay a cutlet on the bed of breadcrumbs. Press it down firmly to crumb it on the first side, then turn it over and to crumb it on the second side. Crumb the sides of the cutlet as well by pressing the crumbs into them. Repeat with all the cutlets, so that they are evenly coated with the breadcrumbs.

9 Heat a medium-sized, non-stick frying pan and add a tsp of refined oil and ½ tsp of butter. Swirl the pan to coat it well.

10 When the oil is hot and the butter has melted, add a couple of breaded cutlets to the pan and fry them, till they are golden and crisp on all sides. Remove and place them on kitchen paper to drain.

11 Add more oil and butter to the pan, as required and fry all the cutlets in the same way.

12 The cutlets should be perfectly cooked through, with the potato holding it together nicely, the delicate taste of the aromatics and spices serving to spruce them perfectly from within.

13 Arrange the fried cutlets on a platter and serve hot with a spicy mint chutney.

Chola Masala
(Spicy Chickpeas and Gram)
8–10 SERVINGS

. . . .

A real Punjabi classic, this is eaten across North India and is cooked with endless variations too. Packed with the goodness of whole Bengal gram and chickpeas, this hearty dish makes for a perfect meal or snack.

Method

1 Wash the chickpeas and gram and soak them in water overnight. Drain and rinse thoroughly, to remove any toxins that may have formed.

2 Parboil the chickpeas and gram in a pressure cooker with 3 cups of water, for 25–30 minutes after the cooker reaches full pressure. They should hold their shape but be soft when mashed with a fork or pressed between the fingers.

3 Transfer them to a bowl and mash them lightly with a fork keeping half of them whole. Set aside.

THE CURRY

4 To make the base for the dish, heat the oil in a wok or kadhai and add the whole spices and bay leaf. Sauté them on medium heat, till they crackle and release their aroma.

5 When the whole spices are nutty and richly coloured, add the onions and sauté for a few minutes, till they turn light golden brown.

6 Stir in the ginger and garlic and sauté, till they are softened and lightly coloured.

7 Sprinkle in the spice powders, salt and sauté for a couple of minutes, till they are aromatic and toasted.

8 Add a few drops of water to deglaze the pan and lift up the spices stuck to the base. Bhuno the masala 3–4 times with water, till the base is homogenous and the oil has risen to the surface.

9 Mix in the cooked chickpeas and gram. Turn up the heat and fry them in the masala base, till they are well coated.

10 Add the tomatoes and continue to fry on high heat, till they begin to disintegrate. Sprinkle in the sugar and mix well to combine.

11 Pour in enough water to come 1" above the contents of the pan. Stir to combine, bring to a boil, turn the heat down and simmer gently for about an hour or more.

12 Cook the chickpeas and gram, till the starch slowly glutenizes with the liquid, so that they are soft and creamy in texture and the gravy thickens.

13 Taste and add a little salt if required.

Ingredients

1 cup of chickpeas
(soaked overnight)

1 cup whole Bengal gram or
kala chana (soaked overnight)

THE CURRY BASE

2 tsp refined oil

1" cassia stick

1 tsp cumin seeds

4–5 cloves

¼ tsp whole black peppercorns

4 green cardamoms

2 brown cardamoms

1 bay leaf

1½ onions, chopped fine

½" ginger, chopped fine

5 garlic cloves, chopped fine

½ tsp turmeric powder

1 tsp red chilli powder

1 tsp coriander powder

A pinch of asafoetida powder

1 tsp salt

3 tomatoes, chopped fine

½ tsp sugar

2 tsp butter

Juice of ½ a lime

2–4 tsp chopped
fresh coriander leaves

14 Once the chola is rich, creamy and aromatic, add the butter and lime juice to lift the flavours.

15 Sprinkle the coriander leaves into the cooked cholas. Mix everything together a few times.

16 Check for a balance of flavours: the chola should be extremely soft and creamy but with a little bite to them and should have the robust taste of the whole spices. The dish should be thick and concentrated in flavour.

17 Serve the chola masala with hot roti, puri or bhatura and a salad.

Easy Fish Cutlets

4 SERVINGS

....

These so-easy-to-make cutlets are the ultimate party or dinner snack. Simply get them ready and chill them in the refrigerator, till your guests arrive. Then fry them in hot oil and serve with a creamy sauce of your liking. Nothing better than freshly made crisp cutlets! Feel free to use any delicate combination of herbs and spices to flavour the cutlets.

Method

1 Cut the fish into fillets, ensuring that all bones have been removed. Wash the fish and drain.

TO STEAM THE FISH

2 Put 2 cups of water into a pan and add the ginger, coriander leaves and chillies to it. Bring the water to a boil and then turn the heat to low. The aromatics and herbs will infuse the water and this will give the fish a delicate aroma when it is steamed over the bubbling water.

3 Put the fish in a steamer basket or colander (instead of a steamer). Place the steamer over the aromatic hot water. Cover and steam for 8–10 minutes on medium heat, till the fish flakes easily when pressed with a fork. Once the fillets are cooked through, remove them from the steamer and set them aside to cool.

THE CUTLETS

4 To make the cutlet mixture, put the cutlet ingredients, except the potatoes into a blender and add a little water. Blitz the ingredients for a couple of minutes and check its consistency. If the mixture appears too dry, add a little more water and blitz it again, till the mixture is wonderfully smooth and quite fine.

5 Now add the steamed fish fillets to the blender and process it, till the mixture has a fine consistency with just a little bit of texture remaining.

6 Remove the mixture to a bowl. Coarsely mash the potatoes and mix them into the cutlet mixture to give it some body and to help bind it with the starch in the potatoes.

7 Taste the mix and stir in more salt if required.

8 Shape the mix into small flat, round cutlets using your hands. Keep a bowl of water on the counter to wet your hands while doing this, to prevent the mixture from sticking, thus making it easier to shape.

9 Once you have shaped all your cutlets, put them on a large tray, cover them and place in the refrigerator to set for about 15 minutes. This keeps the

Ingredients

500 gms any firm-fleshed, white fish	¼" ginger
Refined oil to fry	4–5 garlic cloves
TO STEAM THE FISH	1 green chilli
¼" ginger	A few fresh mint leaves
4–5 fresh coriander sprigs	½ tsp turmeric powder
2 green chillies	½ tsp red chilli powder
THE CUTLETS	½ tsp salt
1 slice of bread	¾ tsp fennel seed powder
1 cup toasted breadcrumbs	½ tsp freshly ground black pepper
1 egg	2 medium-sized potatoes, boiled and peeled

cutlets from breaking apart while frying, as the ingredients bind together well when rested in the refrigerator in this manner.

10 Now, put the oil in a hot non-stick frying pan on medium heat. When the oil is hot, add a couple of cutlets and fry them, till they are deliciously crisp and golden brown on both sides. This should take about 5–6 minutes.

11 Remove them and drain on kitchen paper.

12 Fry all the cutlets, till they are golden brown and have a beautifully crisp crust on the outside.

13 Serve these yummy fish cutlets warm, with a chutney or sauce of your choice.

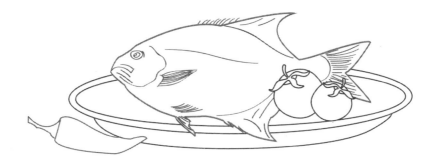

Sweet
RECIPES

Gulab Jamun
Pg 152

Fruit Custard
Pg 146

Badam Kulfi
(Indian Almond Ice Cream)

4 SERVINGS

. . . .

Kulfi is generally referred to as an ice cream, but is more akin to a frozen dessert, being richer and denser in texture. This particular rich, creamy and nutty kulfi is so simple to prepare that after making it for the first time, it becomes a favourite sweet in any menu.

Ingredients

1 cup blanched, peeled and ground almonds

4 tbsp fresh cream

1 cup condensed milk

A pinch of saffron strands

¼ cup milk

A small handful of pistachios

A small handful of almonds, blanched and peeled

Method

1 First, to make to the kulfi mixture, put the ground almonds, cream and condensed milk into a bowl and whisk thoroughly, till it is fully combined and thick.

2 Heat the milk in a small frying pan and when it is almost steaming hot, add the saffron strands to the pan, and let it infuse the milk. Turn off the heat and let the milk cool, stirring it every few minutes.

3 Once the milk has cooled, add it to the kulfi mixture and fold it in to combine well. The ground almonds will act as a thickener and absorb the milk completely. Whisk the mix well, till it is thick, creamy and homogenous.

4 Now, heat a small frying pan and add the almonds and pistachios. Roast them for a few minutes on low to medium heat, till they are nutty and aromatic. Transfer to a chopping board and crush them coarsely with the side of a heavy knife or a rolling pin.

5 Reserve about 2 tbsp of the crushed nuts and add the rest to the kulfi mixture. Stir through to combine. Now the mix is ready for filling into the kulfi moulds or clay kujjas.

6 Spoon the deliciously rich and creamy mixture into each mould, cover with a piece of butter paper and secure with a rubber band stretched around the rim of the mould.

7 Put the mould into the freezer and freeze for 3–4 hours or till the mixture has set perfectly and is hard in texture.

8 Take them out of the refrigerator and remove the butter paper. Dip the moulds into hot water and turn the kulfi out on to a plate. Sprinkle a little of the reserved nuts and serve straight away.

Nariyal Ladoo
(Coconut and Condensed Milk Confectionary)

7–8 SERVINGS

Commonly made in several Indian house-holds for special occasions or even otherwise, fresh home-made coconut ladoos are not only irresistible, but very simple to make. The same recipe can be used with some slight variations to create different versions.

Ingredients

3½ cups grated/desiccated coconut

2 cups condensed milk

2 tbsp crumbled khoya or reduced milk solids

1 tbsp ghee

A few cashewnuts

A few almonds

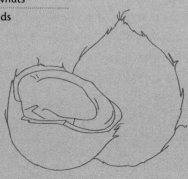

Method

1 Heat a medium-sized kadhai or wok for a couple of minutes on medium heat. Reserve ½ cup of the measured desiccated coconut and add the rest to the kadhai. Dry-roast it for 10–15 minutes, stirring continuously, till it is nutty, sweet and a delicate golden colour. Take care not to singe or burn it.

2 Now add the condensed milk, turn the heat down slightly and stir together well, till the mixture is thick.

3 Add the khoya and continue to cook, till it is completely dissolved and the mixture leaves the sides of the pan. The coconut will also start to release its oils making the mixture quite glossy. Turn off the heat and leave to cool a little.

4 Heat the ghee in a small frying pan and add the nuts. Fry them on low to medium heat, till they are nutty, crunchy and a rich golden colour. Leave them to cool on a chopping board or plate.

5 Line a plate with the reserved ½ cup of desiccated coconut.

6 To make the ladoos, take a little coconut and condensed milk mixture in the palm of one hand and with the other, mould it into the size of a golf ball. Flatten the ball to make a disk. Make a small depression in the centre of the disk with your thumb and put in one cashewnut or almond, pushing it in a little to secure it in the depression.

7 Fold the sides of the disk over the nut in the centre and gently roll it in the palms of your hands to make a perfect round ball once again with the nut enclosed in the centre.

8 Gently roll the ladoo in the desiccated coconut to coat it fully.

9 Repeat the process for the remaining ladoos, about 12 in all.

10 Chill in the refrigerator for about an hour to set.

11 Serve the ladoos cold.

Doodhi ka Halwa
(Bottle Gourd Dessert)

4–5 SERVINGS

A perfect example of how an ordinary vegetable like bottle gourd can be turned into a
rich, caramelized, unusual sweet. This halwa
is really simple to make, but requires patience
to cook the bottle gourd, till it's rich, caramelized and deep reddish-brown in colour. What
is most surprising is the manner in which the
slow caramelization of the gourd intensifies
its flavour, giving the halwa a musky, sweet,
delicate aroma.

Ingredients

3 tbsp ghee

½ a bottle gourd, peeled
and grated

1 cup milk

A few almonds, blanched,
peeled and slivered

¼ cup grated jaggery

Method

1 Heat a deep pan or kadhai and add the ghee.
   Once the ghee is hot and nutty in aroma, add the
   grated bottle gourd and fry it in the ghee on low
   to medium heat, till all its moisture has evaporated and it begins to take on a little colour.

2 Turn the heat down to a simmer and continue to
   cook the bottle gourd, stirring it gently periodically,
   till it turns a rich deep golden brown. The natural
   sugars in the bottle gourd will caramelize slowly and
   smell really nutty and sweet while turning a deep
   golden brown. The process takes about an hour or
   more, so patiently continue to cook and stir gently.

3 While the bottle gourd is on the stove, put the
   milk into a pan and add the slivered almonds.
   Bring the milk to a boil and then simmer it gently
   on low heat, till it is reduced by more than half and
   has turned thick and yellowish with the almonds.
   The almonds will infuse the milk and become really
   soft, thickening the milk in the process. Turn off
   the heat and set aside.

4 Once the bottle gourd is golden brown and the
   ghee starts to release, add the jaggery to the pan
   and mix it in well. Continue cooking the bottle
   gourd and jaggery for another 20 minutes or so,
   till the jaggery is fully dissolved and mixed in.

5 By now, the mixture will be really thick and deep
   golden brown with the caramelized bottle gourd
   and the jaggery.

6 Add the thickened milk and stir it in on low heat,
   till it is fully combined and the bottle gourd is rich
   and creamy in its consistency.

7 Turn off the heat, stir the halwa a few times to
   combine it nicely and serve it piping hot.

Fruit Custard

4–6 SERVINGS

· ·

Good old Indian-style fruit custard is a dessert that count-
less people have grown up with and even today is popular
across the country. Owing to its great popularity, it would
be safe to say that it must be definitely part of India's colo-
nial culinary heritage. One of the little known secrets in
preparing this simple dessert is in making fresh custard;
not using custard powder.

Method

THE FRUIT

1 Chop all the fruit and put them into a bowl. Mix
them gently to get them to start releasing their
juices and squeeze in the lime juice to prevent the
fruit from oxidising and turning brown. Cover and
keep in the refrigerator to chill.

THE CUSTARD

2 To make the custard, pour about 3" of water into a
small pan. Put a glass or metal mixing bowl on top
of the pan to create a double boiler. Put the pan
with the bowl on medium to high heat and bring
the water to a boil. Once the water is boiling and
the steam starts to rise, turn the heat down to a
simmer and keep the water at a gentle boil.

3 Add the egg yolks and sugar to the heated mixing
bowl and start whisking with a balloon whisk, first
gently to combine and then more vigorously, till
the sugar dissolves completely and the egg yolks
are pale yellow and form ribbons when lifted with
a whisk. Turn off the heat and remove the egg yolk
and sugar mixture.

4 Now put the milk and cream into another pan on
low to medium heat for a few minutes, till steam
starts to rise. Stir a few times and turn the heat
down slightly.

5 Add the split vanilla seeds and lightly crushed
cardamoms and leave to infuse over a low simmer
for about 10 minutes.

6 Once the mixture is delicately infused and slightly
reduced, turn off the heat and leave to cool for a
few minutes.

7 Return the egg yolk to the double boiler and turn
on the heat to a low simmer. Add the milk mixture,
a little at a time, whisking gently between each
addition, till well incorporated.

8 Gently cook the egg and milk mixture over the
steam of the double boiler, till the egg yolks start
to cook and the mixture begins to thicken. This is
the most crucial stage for the custard, because if
it gets too hot, the eggs will scramble and the custard will curdle. Therefore, remove the pan from
the heat at the appropriate time.

The Chakh le India Cookbook

Ingredients

THE FRUIT	THE CUSTARD
2 apples, cored and chopped	4 egg yolks, whisked
2 pears, cored and chopped	2–3 tbsp sugar
1½ cups green grapes, halved	400 ml milk
2 bananas, sliced thin	100 ml cream
1 pomegranate, peeled and cleaned	1 fresh vanilla bean, split with seeds scraped out
Any other seasonal fruit such as oranges, strawberries, mangoes, peaches	3 green cardamoms, lightly crushed
Juice of ½ a lime	

9 Once the custard has thickened enough to coat the back of a spoon, and is rich and creamy in texture, take it off the heat and put the base of the bowl into another pan containing a little cold water, to cool it down immediately.

10 Leave it to cool to room temperature, stirring occasionally to prevent a skin from forming on top. Cover the surface of the custard with soft butter paper or cling film and put it into the refrigerator to chill for an hour or so.

TO SERVE

11 Finally, take out both the fruit and the custard from the refrigerator and mix the custard well.

12 Put the fruit into a large serving dish. Pour the chilled custard through a strainer over the fruit.

13 Serve chilled.

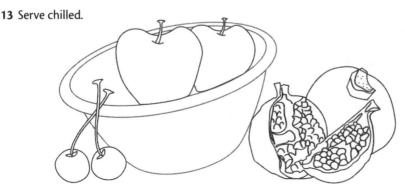

Shrikhand
(Rich Hung Curd Dessert)
4–5 SERVINGS

This creamy sweet-sour, gelato-like sweet, filled with the goodness of hung curd, is one of the best known desserts from Maharashtra. It has to be one of the simplest and quickest Indian sweets to make. It's light and fluffy and a delight to eat when served chilled.

Ingredients

| ¼ cup milk |
| A few saffron strands |
| 2 cups hung curd |
| 1½ tbsp castor sugar |
| 10–12 pistachios, toasted and chopped |
| 10–12 almonds, toasted and slivered |

Method

1 Put the milk in a small frying pan on medium heat, till it is almost boiling and then turn off the heat. Add the saffron and stir it in. Leave the milk to infuse, till it is scented a light yellow.

2 Put the hung curd into a bowl and add the sugar. Whisk till the sugar is well blended into the curd.

3 Throw in most of the chopped nuts (reserving a little for decoration) and add the saffron-infused milk to the bowl. Gently fold them into the mix and then whisk it a few times to combine completely.

4 Continue to whisk the mixture, till it turns pale lemon yellow, light and smooth.

5 Check for a balance of flavours: it should be mildly sweet, with the flavour of the saffron coming through delicately. The hung curd should give it that essential sour, delicious twang on the finish, with the nuts providing a slight crunch in between. The consistency should be that of a rich butter frosting, but a little more pourable, light and fluffy, so do not over-whisk the mixture.

6 Now, spoon the creamy, fresh, hung curd-based mixture into dessert bowls, sprinkle the reserved chopped nuts on top and put it into the refrigerator to chill for a few hours.

7 Serve chilled.

Nariyal Ladoo
Pg 144

Shahi Tukda
Pg 157

Seviyan
Pg 156

Shrikhand
Pg 148

Phirni

(Almond and Pistachio Ground Rice Custard)

4 SERVINGS

Phirni is one of my favourite Indian desserts as it's light and creamy, with the nuts and cardamom, and makes for the perfect dessert after a North Indian feast. It should be made much in advance and always served chilled as its flavour matures after a few hours of chilling. It is traditionally set and served in individual earthenware cups and tastes best that way.

Ingredients

1 cup milk
2 tbsp rice flour
1½ tbsp sugar
A small handful of almonds
A small handful of pistachios
2–3 green cardamoms, seeds only

Method

1. Heat a deep pan on low heat for a minute and add the milk. Bring the milk to a gentle boil.

2. Now whisk the rice flour gently into the hot milk. While whisking the milk and flour, ensure that no lumps are formed and the flour completely dissolves into the milk to make the phirni soft and consistent.

3. Add the sugar and continue to whisk on low heat, till the sugar dissolves completely. As the starch in the rice flour begins to gluttonize, the mixture will thicken and soon coat the back of the spoon. At this stage, it should have the consistency of condensed milk. Turn off the heat.

4. Slice the nuts into thin slivers and grind the cardamom seeds to a semi-fine powder. Add most of the nuts, reserving a few pieces for decoration. Add most of the cardamom powder to give the phirni a delicate fragrance.

5. Turn on the heat but keep it low and gently whisk the thick mixture for 5–7 minutes to amalgamate all the flavours fully.

6. Now turn off the heat and let the mixture cool for about 10 minutes, stirring periodically to prevent a skin from forming on the surface.

7. Spoon the mixture into glass or earthenware cups. Sprinkle the reserved chopped nuts and cardamom powder on top.

8. Place the phirni in the refrigerator for 3–4 hours, till it is perfectly set and chilled.

9. Serve cold.

Gulab Jamun

6–8 SERVINGS

. . . .

This is one of India's favourite sweets, cutting across all regions. Hot gulab jamuns on a cold winter night is about as close to dessert nirvana as it gets. This dessert does require some practise but can be made perfectly with this recipe. As an add-on, try stuffing each jamun with a nut for a little crunchy surprise on the inside.

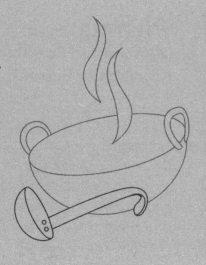

Method

THE JAMUNS

1 The first step is to make the jamuns. Put the soft, moist khoya into a bowl and add 2 tbsp of flour to it. Work in the flour with your hands and knead it to make a soft dough. Add a little more flour if the dough is too loose and not holding together.

2 Knead the mixture gently, till it forms a smooth, pliable dough. Now, take a little dough in your hands and roll it into the size of a golf ball, gently between the cupped palms of your hands. Place the jamun on a lightly floured plate.

3 Repeat with the remaining dough. There should be around a dozen or so, depending on the size.

THE CHAASHNI

4 To make the chaashni, which in this case is a rose-and-saffron-infused thick sugar syrup. Put the sugar into a pan with 2½ cups of water and bring to a boil, stirring to dissolve the sugar.

5 When the sugar has dissolved completely, turn the heat down and simmer, till the syrup begins to thicken a little.

6 Add the cardamoms, saffron strands and rose water and stir well to mix. Continue to simmer the syrup, till it begins to coat the back of a spoon.

7 The syrup will have a delicate and exotic fragrance with the aromatic cardamom and saffron and the perfume of the rose water. Once the syrup is a rich saffron in colour and quite syrupy and reduced, turn off the heat and leave to infuse.

TO FRY AND SERVE THE JAMUNS

8 Next, deep fry the jamuns. Heat the oil in a kadhai on medium heat and add a 1" cube of bread to test the temperature of the oil. If the bread starts to brown evenly and turns golden in about a minute or so, the oil is at the perfect temperature. If it browns and burns very quickly, it's too hot.

9 The temperature of the oil is very important here, as the jamuns need to be deep-fried on steady heat. They should cook all the way through inside while turning a deep golden brown on the outside.

10 Once the oil is the right temperature, add the jamuns and deep-fry them gently, till fully cooked

Ingredients

THE JAMUNS

2 cups crumbled, soft, moist
    khoya or reduced milk solids

3–4 tbsp refined flour

Refined oil to deep-fry the jamuns

THE CHAASHNI

400 gms sugar

2 green cardamoms

A pinch of saffron strands

1 tsp rose water

and golden brown. Remove them with a slotted
spoon and drain on kitchen paper.

11 Once all the jamuns are fried and golden, turn off
the heat and carefully transfer the hot oil to a heat
proof container. Now put the infused syrup on low
heat and bring it to a very slow simmer.

12 Add the fried jamuns and gently poach them in
the sugar syrup, till they are meltingly soft and
have soaked up all the syrup.

13 Serve them hot.

Aam ki Kheer
(Mango Rice Pudding)
8–10 SERVINGS

....

As large varieties of mangoes are found in India, this sweet is particularly fascinating—a perfect mix of the "king of fruits" and rice. Unlike other kheers which can also be served hot, this variation should only be served chilled and is a great dessert for summer. The starch in the rice is released slowly while cooking, making the kheer creamy and lush even while retaining the aroma of the mangoes.

Method

1 Wash the rice thoroughly and drain it.

2 Heat a deep pan on low heat for a couple of minutes. Add 2 cups of the milk and the rice and stir them well together.

3 Add the sugar, mix it in properly and turn up the heat to bring the mixture to a gentle boil, stirring occasionally.

4 Once the milk begins to boil, turn the heat down to a bare simmer. Stir the rice a few times, cover the pan and let the rice cook in the milk, till it is soft, mushy and breaking apart.

5 When the rice has released most of its starch into the milk and the mixture is thick, add a little of the measured milk. Stir it through to combine, cover the pan and continue to cook the rice, till it is over-cooked, but still holding some of its shape.

6 The entire process up to this stage takes about 45 minutes, but that could vary depending on the variety of rice.

7 Now, add the fresh mango purée or canned pulp. Stir it in gently to combine, till the kheer turns yellow in colour.

8 Add the saffron, almonds and soaked and drained raisins. Mix them together and simmer the kheer for another 2 hours or so, stirring it every 20 minutes and adding a little more of the measured milk to keep it moist and creamy.

9 Stir in the cardamoms about 15 minutes before removing the pan from the heat.

10 Cooking the kheer slowly on very low heat is essential, as the starch in the rice is gently coaxed out into the milk, giving it a creamy texture. It will continue to thicken the kheer as more and more starch is released into the milk. So the longer it cooks, the better, provided that the rice doesn't become a paste. It's like cooking a risotto, only this takes slightly longer. Adding a little milk periodically is essential to prevent the kheer from drying out and burning.

11 Once the kheer is cooked, creamy and a rich mango and saffron yellow, stir it a few times to help the rice release more of its starch. Turn off the heat.

12 Check for a balance of flavours: the kheer should be delicately infused with the mangoes and saffron, the rice should be mushy, but with a hint of

Ingredients

- 1 cup long-grained rice
- 2½ cups milk
- 3 tbsp sugar
- 3 fresh ripe mangoes, puréed or 1 cup canned mango pulp
- A pinch of saffron strands
- A small handful of almonds, toasted and chopped
- A small handful of seedless raisins, soaked in water for 15 minutes
- 4 green cardamoms
- Melted butter to coat the kheer

a bite to it. Overall, the kheer should be thick and creamy; the nuts and raisins juicy and semi-soft, giving the dish a little textural contrast.

13 Once the kheer is cool, spoon it into individual dessert bowls or a large serving bowl. Cover it with a thin film of melted butter, to prevent a thick skin forming on the surface.

14 Put the kheer into the refrigerator to chill for a few hours and to mature.

15 Remove the layer of butter with the tip of a knife.

16 Serve chilled.

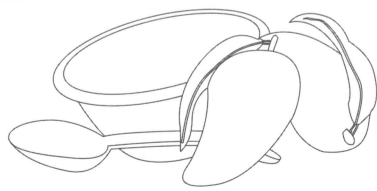

Seviyan
(Vermicelli Dessert)

4–6 SERVINGS

There are few Indian desserts or sweets that can measure up to a bowl of chilled, home-made seviyan. It's rich and creamy, delicately aromatic and is the perfect way to end a traditional Indian meal.

Ingredients

2 tbsp ghee

250 gms vermicelli

¼ cup cashewnuts

¼ cup almonds

¼ cup seedless raisins

2¾ cups milk

2 tbsp sugar

4 green cardamoms

DECORATION

2 tsp chopped cashewnuts and almonds

Method

1 First, to fry the vermicelli, heat the ghee in a medium-sized frying pan. Break the strands of vermicelli in half and add them to the pan. Fry for a few minutes on low to medium heat, till they turn light golden.

2 Break up the nuts with a heavy knife or rolling pin and add them to the pan along with the raisins. Fry the nuts and raisins with the vermicelli to gently toast them and intensify their nuttiness.

3 When the nuts and vermicelli turn golden, turn off the heat and set the pan aside.

4 Now, heat a deep pan for a minute or so and pour in the milk. Add the sugar and bring the milk to a boil on high heat. Add the cardamoms to infuse the milk with their flavour.

5 Simmer the milk on medium heat, till it is reduced by half and begins to thicken.

6 Now, break up the vermicelli into small pieces or fragments and add them to the simmering milk along with the nuts and raisins.

7 Stir everything together to combine well and simmer the vermicelli, stirring gently every few minutes, till the mixture is thick and creamy and the vermicelli and nuts are soft with the mildly-sweet, cardamom-infused milk.

8 Stir the cooked vermicelli a few times more to combine, turn off the heat and leave the thick and creamy seviyan to cool.

9 It should have the consistency of a rice pudding. The vermicelli will release its starch into the milk, turning it thick and creamy as it simmers away gently. You can add a little more milk if the mixture gets too thick.

10 Once the seviyan has cooled, put it into the refrigerator to chill for a couple of hours.

11 Serve the vermicelli dessert chilled, in small bowls or cups, sprinkled with chopped nuts.

Shahi Tukda

(Fried Bread in a Reduced Milk and Saffron Sauce)

4 SERVINGS

Shahi tukda literally means "royal pieces". Traced back to Mughal times, it's a wonderfully simple yet elegant dessert made with fried bread soaked in a thick and sweet milk sauce. The crisp bread and rich creamy sauce is a great combination and to add to the flavour, it's sprinkled and infused with rose water and saffron.

Ingredients

THE MILK SYRUP

2 cups milk

1½ tbsp sugar

A few saffron strands

THE BREAD

4 slices white bread

3–4 tsp refined oil

Method

THE MILK SYRUP

1 First, put the milk into a pan and add the sugar. Bring it up to a boil on high heat.

2 Turn the heat down and add the saffron strands. Simmer the milk on very low heat, even as the saffron gets infused into it.

3 Continue to simmer the milk, till it is reduced to the consistency of a thick saffron-yellow cream, stirring it frequently, to prevent the sugar in the milk from sticking to the bottom. Turn off the heat, stir the thickened milky syrup a few times and set it aside, covered and warm.

THE BREAD

4 Now, cut off the crusts of the bread slices and discard them. Cut each slice into 2 triangles through the centre.

5 Heat a medium-sized frying pan and add the oil. Swirl the pan to coat it well and add the bread triangles to the pan. Fry them on medium heat, till they are crisp and golden brown on both sides.

6 Drain the fried bread triangles on kitchen paper to absorb excess oil.

TO SERVE

7 Next, transfer the crisp, golden, fried bread triangles to a serving platter or dish. Stir the warm, thickened, saffron milk sauce a couple of times and pour it over the fried bread, covering each triangle fully.

8 Allow the bread to soak up some of the milk sauce for a couple of minutes and then serve.